Dexter

Life and Training

SOUTHERLAND | COPYRIGHT 2023

Contents

Contents 2

Introduction 7

Early Life 8

Rise to Prominence 8

Championship Years 10

Overcoming Adversity 11

The Later Years and Evolution 12

Legacy and Influence 13

Life Beyond Bodybuilding 14

The Dexter Jackson Training Philosophy 15

Workout Routines 16

Advanced Training Techniques 20

Overcoming Injuries and Setbacks 21

Pre-Competition Preparation 22

The Importance of Nutrition in Bodybuilding 24

Dexter Jackson's Diet Plan 25

Meal Frequency and Timing 26

Macronutrient Balance 27

Meal Preparation and Planning 29

Supplements in Dexter's Regimen 30

Adapting Nutrition for Different Phases 31

Dexter's Day-to-Day 32

Building a Legacy 34

Conclusion 35

Introduction to Bodybuilding Techniques 36

Understanding Muscle Growth 40

Giant Sets 41

Super Sets 43

Forced Reps 44

Eccentric Contractions (Negatives) 46

Twenty-Ones 47

Timed Sets/Reps 49

Partial Reps 50

Pre-Exhaustion 52

Post-Exhaustion Sets 53

Pyramiding 54

Advanced Training Techniques 55

Workout Schedules and Routines 58

Personalizing Your Workout 60

Workout Splits Introduction 61

The Essence of Workout Splits 64

The Science Behind Splitting Workouts... 67

Tailoring Your Split: Factors to Consider 69

A Balanced Approach: Combining Science with Individual Needs 71

The Full Body Split... 72

    Example Full Body Workout Routines 77

        Beginner Routine 77

        Intermediate Routine... 78

        Advanced Routine 78

The Upper/Lower Split... 79

    Example Upper and Lower Body Workouts............................... 81

        Upper Body Routine.. 82

        Lower Body Routine.. 83

        Advanced Options 83

        Ideal Candidates for the Upper/Lower Split 84

    Example upper/lower split workouts 86

Push/Pull/Legs Split... 88

    Push Workout 90

    Pull Workout... 91

- Legs Workout 92
  - Ideal Candidates for the Push/Pull/Legs Split 93
- The Bro Split 94
  - Example Workout Routine 96
  - Ideal Candidates for the Bro Split 99
- The 5x5 Split 100
  - Example 5x5 Workouts 102
  - Benefits of Strength-Focused Splits 105
- Hybrid and Custom Splits 107
  - Examples of Hybrid Splits 110
  - The Benefits of Personalized Splits 112
  - Ideal Candidates for Hybrid and Custom Splits 114
- Navigating the Complexities of Workout Splits 115
  - Frequently Asked Questions 115
  - Debunking Common Misconceptions 116
  - Tips to Avoid Common Mistakes in Workout Splits 117
  - Fine-Tuning Your Workout Split 118
  - Incorporating Feedback into Your Routine 118
- Nutrition for Optimal Performance 118
- Macronutrients for Muscle Growth 122

Micronutrients and Supplements 126

Meal Planning and Timing 131

Nutritional Strategies for Bulking and Cutting 138

Specialized Diets for Bodybuilders..142

Staying Hydrated and Monitoring Progress....................................146

Example Meal Plans 153

    Meal Plan 1: Fuel for Bulking 153

    Meal Plan 2: Precision for Cutting...154

    Meal Plan 3: Vegetarian Power..156

Common Mistakes and Pitfalls 157

Mental and Emotional Aspects..162

Embracing Your Fitness Journey 165

Introduction

Dexter Jackson, born on November 25, 1969, in Jacksonville, Florida, stands as one of the most decorated bodybuilders in history. Known for his remarkable consistency and longevity in the sport, Jackson's career is marked by a record-setting 29 IFBB professional bodybuilding wins, a feat unrivaled in the history of the sport. His crowning achievement came in 2008 when he won the Mr. Olympia title, bodybuilding's most prestigious award. "Winning the Mr. Olympia was a dream come true, something I'd been working towards my entire career," Jackson remarked on his triumph (Muscle & Fitness, 2008). His physique, characterized by its aesthetic symmetry and detailed muscularity, set a new standard in bodybuilding, challenging the prevailing trends of size and mass dominance.

Dexter's career extended well beyond what is typical in the demanding world of professional bodybuilding. He competed at the highest levels into his 50s, a testament to his rigorous training ethic and smart approach to body maintenance. "It's all about listening to your body and adapting. That's how you last in this sport," Jackson explained (Flex Magazine, 2015). His ability to stay injury-free and consistently present a top-tier physique at competitions underscored his mastery of the sport.

Jackson's influence extended beyond the stage, as he became a role model and mentor for aspiring bodybuilders, sharing his knowledge and experiences. He was not just a champion but an ambassador for bodybuilding, representing the sport with dignity and inspiring a generation of athletes to pursue their bodybuilding aspirations with dedication and discipline.

Early Life

Growing up in a modest family environment, Jackson's early life was far from the glitz and glamour of the bodybuilding stages he would later dominate. Sports were a significant part of his upbringing, with a young Dexter showing a keen interest in football and track. These early athletic endeavors laid the foundation for his exceptional discipline and work ethic. "I was always competitive, always wanted to be the best at whatever I did," Jackson recalled about his youthful pursuits (Bodybuilding.com Interview, 2010).

It was during his teenage years that Jackson stumbled upon the world of bodybuilding. Initially, his interest was sparked not by a desire to compete but by a simple goal: to gain strength and size for football. This casual interest, however, quickly turned into a passion. He was drawn to the discipline and the transformative nature of bodybuilding. "Once I started lifting, I just fell in love with how my body changed and how I felt," he shared in an interview (Iron Magazine, 2012).

By the time he was 20, Jackson had fully immersed himself in the sport, participating in local bodybuilding contests. These early competitions were more than just a platform for him to showcase his growing physique; they were a learning ground where Jackson began to hone the skills and techniques that would later define his career. His family, although initially unfamiliar with the sport, soon became his steadfast supporters, witnessing his transformation from a local gym enthusiast to a promising bodybuilding talent.

Rise to Prominence

Dexter Jackson's rise in the bodybuilding world was a blend of relentless hard work and strategic mastery of the sport. After his initial forays into local competitions, where he quickly made a name for himself, Jackson set his sights on larger stages. His first significant breakthrough came in 1992 when he won the light-heavyweight title at the NPC Southern States Championship. This victory was not just a trophy; it was a validation of his potential. "That win was when I knew I could really make a mark in this sport," Jackson reflected (Flex Magazine Interview, 1993).

The challenges in these early stages of his career were numerous. Dexter had to balance rigorous training with financial constraints, often having to work multiple jobs to fund his bodybuilding aspirations. "There were times it was tough, but my passion for bodybuilding kept me going," he stated (Muscle & Fitness Interview, 1994). His dedication paid off when he earned his IFBB Pro card in 1998 after winning the North American Championships. This was a turning point, marking his entry into the professional league.

In the professional arena, Jackson quickly distinguished himself. Despite competing against more seasoned and often bigger bodybuilders, his exceptional symmetry, conditioning, and presentation skills caught the attention of judges and fans alike. His first professional win came at the 2002 Night of Champions, a victory that propelled him into the upper echelons of the sport. Jackson's philosophy of prioritizing conditioning over sheer size was contrary to the trend of the era, yet it was this approach that set him apart. "I wanted to be known for my aesthetics and conditioning, not just for being big," he explained (Ironman Magazine, 2002).

Jackson's ascension continued with consistent placements at top shows, including the prestigious Mr. Olympia. His steady rise was a testament to his methodical approach and unwavering focus. He wasn't just participating; he was reshaping the expectations and standards of professional bodybuilding.

Championship Years

Dexter Jackson's championship years were marked by a series of remarkable achievements that firmly established him as one of the greats in bodybuilding. The pinnacle of his career came in 2008 when he clinched the Mr. Olympia title, bodybuilding's most coveted prize. This victory was not only a personal triumph but also a moment of historical significance in the sport. "Winning Mr. Olympia was not just about the title. It was about proving that aesthetics and symmetry could triumph over sheer size," Jackson stated (Muscle & Fitness, 2008).

The preparation for each competition during these years was an exercise in precision and discipline. Jackson's routine was meticulous, involving rigorous training, strict dieting, and an unwavering commitment to excellence. "Every competition I entered, I aimed to be better than the last. That meant pushing harder each time," he said (Flex Magazine, 2009). His ability to consistently bring an improved package to each show set him apart from his competitors.

In addition to his Mr. Olympia win, Jackson amassed an impressive array of titles, including multiple Arnold Classic wins, a feat that underscored his dominance in the sport. Each victory was a testament to his relentless pursuit of perfection. "The Arnold Classic wins were special because they showed consistency at the highest level of the sport," Jackson noted (Bodybuilding.com, 2013).

Throughout these championship years, Jackson's approach to bodybuilding evolved. He demonstrated an extraordinary capacity to adapt his training and nutrition strategies to maintain his edge over younger competitors. This adaptability was key to his longevity and success. "Adaptation and evolution were crucial. As the sport changed, so did I," he emphasized (Ironman Magazine, 2010).

Jackson's championship years were not merely a collection of titles and trophies; they were a reflection of his dedication, resilience, and mastery of the art and science of bodybuilding.

Overcoming Adversity

Dexter Jackson's career, though illustrious, was not without its share of adversity. Injuries and losses were part of his journey, each posing a significant challenge to his aspirations and momentum. Despite these setbacks, Jackson's resilience and strategic approach to overcoming obstacles defined his career as much as his victories.

One of the most significant challenges came in the form of injuries. Bodybuilding, by its very nature, places immense strain on the body, and Jackson was not immune to this. He faced several injuries throughout his career, including issues with his back and joints. However, Jackson viewed these setbacks not as roadblocks but as learning opportunities. "Injuries teach you about your body's limits. It's about how you respond to them that defines you as an athlete," he said (Flex Magazine, 2007).

Difficult losses also marked Jackson's career. Not every competition resulted in a win, and some of these losses were deeply disappointing. However, Jackson used these experiences to fuel his determination rather than dampen his spirit. "You learn more from the losses than the wins. They push you to work harder and come back stronger," he reflected (Muscle & Fitness, 2010).

To overcome these challenges, Jackson employed a combination of smart training modifications and mental fortitude. He adapted his workouts to accommodate and recover from injuries, showing a remarkable ability to listen to his body and adjust accordingly. His mental resilience was equally critical; maintaining a positive outlook and a focus on long-term goals helped him navigate through tough times.

Jackson's approach to adversity significantly shaped his career and personal growth. Each challenge reinforced his commitment to the sport and deepened his understanding of his body's capabilities. This resilience not only contributed to his longevity in bodybuilding but also served as an inspiration to others in the sport. "It's not just about building muscles, it's about building character," Jackson aptly summarized (Bodybuilding.com, 2012).

The Later Years and Evolution

As Dexter Jackson progressed into the later years of his career, his role in the bodybuilding community underwent a significant transformation. While continuing to compete at a high level, Jackson gradually shifted his focus towards mentoring and guiding upcoming bodybuilders, sharing the wisdom garnered from decades of experience. "It's about giving back to the sport that has given me so much," Jackson expressed (Iron Magazine, 2018).

Adapting his training and lifestyle with age was crucial for Jackson. He recognized the importance of evolving his approach to maintain peak physical condition while safeguarding his health. This evolution involved more attention to recovery, a refined nutritional strategy, and a training regimen that was rigorous yet mindful of the limitations that come with age. "As you get older, training smarter is just as important as training harder," he mentioned in an interview (Flex Magazine, 2017).

Jackson's contributions extended beyond his own physical training. He became a mentor and a source of inspiration for younger athletes, often providing advice on training techniques, competition preparation, and career management. His involvement in various bodybuilding seminars and workshops allowed him to directly impact the next generation of bodybuilders. "Seeing young athletes grow and succeed in this sport, knowing I played a part in that, is incredibly rewarding," Jackson said (Bodybuilding.com, 2019).

In these later years, Dexter Jackson not only continued to cement his legacy as a top competitor but also solidified his role as a pillar of the bodybuilding community. His commitment to nurturing new talent and sharing his vast knowledge became as much a part of his legacy as his numerous titles and accolades.

Legacy and Influence

Dexter Jackson's impact on the world of bodybuilding is profound and multifaceted. Known for his longevity, consistency, and a remarkable record of victories, his legacy extends far beyond the trophies and titles. He fundamentally influenced the sport's practices, culture, and the standards by which bodybuilders are judged. "Dexter redefined what it meant to be a successful bodybuilder. His emphasis on symmetry and aesthetics over sheer size shifted the sport's trajectory," noted a fellow competitor (Flex Magazine, 2020).

Peers and experts in the field often cite Jackson's career as a benchmark for professionalism and excellence. His approach to training, nutrition, and competition prep has been emulated by many up-and-coming athletes. "He set a new standard, showing us that with the right approach, one can have a long and successful career in bodybuilding," a renowned bodybuilding coach mentioned (Muscle & Fitness, 2021).

Younger athletes, in particular, look up to Jackson not just for his achievements but for the character he displayed throughout his career. His work ethic, resilience in the face of adversity, and willingness to adapt and evolve are often highlighted as sources of inspiration. "Dexter's career taught me that with dedication and smart training, the possibilities in this sport are limitless," shared an emerging bodybuilding talent (Bodybuilding.com, 2022).

Jackson's influence also permeates the cultural aspects of bodybuilding. He is celebrated for his sportsmanship, humility, and the respect he commands from both competitors and fans. His contributions to the sport's growth, including his mentoring and advocacy for bodybuilders' wellbeing, are widely acknowledged.

In summary, Dexter Jackson's legacy in bodybuilding is characterized not only by his impressive competitive record but also by his impact on the sport's evolution and the positive influence he has had on its community. His career serves as a template for success, longevity, and influence in the highly competitive world of bodybuilding.

Life Beyond Bodybuilding

Dexter Jackson's life beyond the gym is as rich and varied as his career in bodybuilding. Away from the weights and the spotlight, he engages in a range of activities that showcase his diverse interests and commitments. "Bodybuilding is a huge part of my life, but it's not my whole life," Jackson shared in an interview (Men's Health, 2020).

Family plays a central role in Jackson's life. He often speaks about the grounding and support his family provides, a stark contrast to the solitary nature of bodybuilding. "My family keeps me balanced. They're my biggest fans and my greatest support system," he stated (Muscle Insider, 2018). Balancing the demands of a professional bodybuilding career with family life is challenging, but Jackson has always prioritized his role as a father and husband.

Outside of his family and training, Jackson has ventured into various business endeavors related to fitness and nutrition. He has leveraged his experience and knowledge to develop training programs, dietary supplements, and fitness apparel. These ventures not only extend his influence in the fitness world but also showcase his entrepreneurial spirit. "I wanted to create products and programs that reflect what

I've learned over the years – to help others achieve their fitness goals," Jackson explained (Flex Magazine, 2019).

Jackson's hobbies and interests outside of bodybuilding are diverse. He enjoys cars, particularly customizing and collecting them, a hobby that allows him to express his creativity and technical interest. Additionally, he is an avid fan of various sports, often found cheering on his favorite teams when not in the gym.

In essence, Dexter Jackson's life beyond bodybuilding is a testament to his multifaceted personality. His commitments as a family man, entrepreneur, and hobbyist offer a glimpse into the man behind the muscle, providing a fuller understanding of one of bodybuilding's greatest athletes.

The Dexter Jackson Training Philosophy

Dexter Jackson's training philosophy is grounded in a trio of core principles: discipline, consistency, and a strong mindset. These tenets have not only defined his approach to bodybuilding but have also distinguished him in a sport often dominated by ever-changing trends and methodologies. "My philosophy is simple – stay disciplined, be consistent, and always keep a strong mind," Jackson stated (Bodybuilding.com, 2016).

Discipline, for Jackson, meant unwavering adherence to his training and diet regimes. He approached each workout with a meticulous plan, ensuring that every exercise, rep, and set was executed with purpose. This discipline extended to his diet, which he managed with precision, understanding its crucial role in sculpting his award-winning physique. "You can't out-train a bad diet, and you can't achieve anything in this sport without discipline," he often remarked (Flex Magazine, 2014).

Consistency was another cornerstone of Jackson's training philosophy. He believed in the power of maintaining a steady, dedicated approach to training, rather than seeking quick fixes or jumping between different routines. This consistency was evident in his longevity in the sport, competing at the highest levels well into his 50s. "Consistency is key. It's about showing up day after day, year after year, and doing the work," Jackson emphasized (Muscle & Fitness, 2017).

Jackson's strong mindset set him apart from many of his peers. Bodybuilding is as much a mental game as it is physical, and Jackson's mental toughness and positive attitude were critical to his success. He approached challenges with a problem-solving mindset and remained focused on his goals, regardless of obstacles. "Bodybuilding is tough, mentally and physically. You have to be strong in both to succeed," he acknowledged (Ironman Magazine, 2015).

Jackson's training philosophy differed from conventional wisdom in its emphasis on sustainability and balance. While the trend in bodybuilding often leaned towards maximal size and mass, Jackson focused on achieving a balanced, aesthetic physique. This approach not only earned him accolades but also contributed to his longevity in the sport.

In summary, Dexter Jackson's training philosophy is a testament to the power of discipline, consistency, and a strong mindset. His unique approach, focusing on sustainable practices and mental toughness, has not only

Workout Routines

Dexter Jackson's workout routines reflect a blend of intensity, variety, and strategic planning, tailored to maximize muscle growth and definition. His weekly training split typically involved targeting different muscle groups on separate days, allowing for focused training and adequate recovery. "Each muscle group gets my full attention. It's about quality, not just quantity," Jackson explained (Muscle & Fitness, 2018).

A typical week in Jackson's training regime might look like this:

- Monday: Chest - Focused on compound movements like bench presses and incline presses, complemented by isolation exercises such as flyes. "The key is to start heavy for strength and finish with lighter, high-rep sets for definition," he said (Flex Magazine, 2016).

- Tuesday: Back - A mix of width and thickness exercises, including pull-ups, rows, and deadlifts. Jackson emphasized the importance of varying grip and angle to target different areas of the back.

- Wednesday: Shoulders - Shoulder workouts involved a combination of presses and lateral raises, aiming to build both mass and symmetry. "Shoulders are critical for that V-taper look," Jackson noted (Bodybuilding.com, 2017).

- Thursday: Legs - Leg days were split between quads and hamstrings. Squats, leg presses, and lunges for quads; leg curls and stiff-leg deadlifts for hamstrings. "Legs are the foundation. I train them hard and heavy," Jackson stated (Ironman Magazine, 2018).

- Friday: Arms - A mix of bicep and tricep exercises, including curls and tricep pushdowns. "I aim for a balance between biceps and triceps to create a harmonious arm development," he mentioned (Muscle Insider, 2019).

- Saturday and Sunday: Rest and Recovery - Rest days were crucial for muscle growth and recovery. Jackson used these days for light cardio, stretching, and recuperation.

Jackson's exercise selection and sequencing were designed to maximize muscle stimulation and growth. He believed in starting workouts with compound movements to engage multiple muscle groups and generate overall strength, followed by isolation exercises for targeted muscle development. "It's about hitting the muscles from every angle," he often said (Flex Magazine, 2020).

Adapting Jackson's routines to individual fitness levels and goals involves understanding one's own body and limitations. Beginners might reduce the intensity and volume, focusing on mastering form before progressing to heavier weights. More advanced lifters could follow Jackson's routines more closely, adjusting as necessary based on their own response and recovery.

Here is an example of a weekly workout split including exercises, sets, and reps:

Monday: Chest

- Bench Press: 4 sets of 6-8 reps
- Incline Dumbbell Press: 4 sets of 8-10 reps
- Machine Chest Press: 3 sets of 10-12 reps
- Cable Flyes: 3 sets of 12-15 reps
- Dips: 3 sets to failure

Tuesday: Back

- Wide-Grip Pull-Ups: 4 sets of 8-10 reps
- Bent Over Rows: 4 sets of 6-8 reps
- Deadlifts: 3 sets of 6-8 reps
- Lat Pull-Downs: 3 sets of 10-12 reps

- Seated Cable Rows: 3 sets of 10-12 reps

Wednesday: Shoulders

- Military Press: 4 sets of 6-8 reps
- Side Lateral Raises: 4 sets of 10-12 reps
- Front Dumbbell Raises: 3 sets of 10-12 reps
- Rear Delt Flyes: 3 sets of 12-15 reps
- Shrugs: 3 sets of 8-10 reps

Thursday: Legs

- Squats: 4 sets of 6-8 reps
- Leg Press: 4 sets of 10-12 reps
- Walking Lunges: 3 sets of 12 reps per leg
- Leg Curls: 4 sets of 10-12 reps
- Stiff-Leg Deadlifts: 3 sets of 10-12 reps
- Seated Calf Raises: 4 sets of 15-20 reps

Friday: Arms

- Barbell Curls: 4 sets of 8-10 reps
- Tricep Pushdowns: 4 sets of 10-12 reps
- Hammer Curls: 3 sets of 10-12 reps
- Skull Crushers: 3 sets of 8-10 reps
- Concentration Curls: 3 sets of 12-15 reps

- Overhead Tricep Extension: 3 sets of 10-12 reps

Saturday and Sunday: Rest and Recovery

- Active Recovery: Light cardio, stretching, and mobility exercises.
- Focus on adequate nutrition and hydration for muscle repair and growth.

This workout split is a balanced approach reflecting Dexter Jackson's training style, focusing on muscle group-specific exercises, a mix of compound and isolation movements, and a range of rep schemes to promote both strength and muscle hypertrophy. It's important for individuals to adjust the weights, sets, and reps according to their own fitness levels and recovery capabilities.

Dexter Jackson's workout routines are a masterclass in bodybuilding training. They exemplify a deep understanding of muscle mechanics and demonstrate how strategic exercise selection and sequencing can lead to optimal muscle development.

Advanced Training Techniques

Dexter Jackson's regimen includes several advanced training techniques that have been integral to his success. These methods are designed to push the body's limits and break through plateaus, ensuring continuous progress and development.

One key technique in Jackson's arsenal is "Pyramid Sets." This involves gradually increasing the weight while decreasing the reps over successive sets. For example, in a bench press, he might start with a lighter weight for 12 reps, increase the weight for 10 reps, and continue this pattern, culminating in a heavy set of 6 reps. "Pyramid sets help in building both strength and muscle endurance," Jackson explained (Muscle & Fitness, 2016).

Jackson also frequently employs "Supersets," where he performs two exercises back-to-back with no rest in between. This could involve working the same muscle group with different exercises or targeting opposing muscle groups. For instance, a bicep curl immediately followed by a tricep extension. "Supersets are great for increasing intensity and endurance in your workouts," he noted (Flex Magazine, 2017).

Another advanced technique is "Drop Sets." Here, Jackson would perform an exercise until failure, then quickly reduce the weight and continue to do more reps until failure is reached again. This method is particularly effective in achieving muscle hypertrophy. "Drop sets force your muscles to adapt and grow. They're tough, but incredibly effective," he shared (Bodybuilding.com, 2018).

To safely incorporate these advanced techniques, Jackson advises starting with lighter weights to understand the body's response. Proper form and controlled movements are crucial to prevent injury. He also stresses the importance of listening to one's body and allowing adequate recovery time. "It's about pushing your limits, but also knowing them," he said (Ironman Magazine, 2019).

Dexter Jackson's advanced training techniques are powerful tools for those looking to elevate their workouts. Proper implementation of these methods can lead to significant gains in strength, endurance, and muscle size, helping individuals break through plateaus and achieve new levels of fitness.

Overcoming Injuries and Setbacks

Dexter Jackson's career, marked by remarkable achievements, also faced its share of injuries and setbacks, a common aspect of high-level bodybuilding. His approach to these challenges was marked by resilience and adaptability, essential qualities for any athlete, especially in a sport as physically demanding as bodybuilding.

Injuries were an inevitable part of Jackson's journey. He faced various physical setbacks, including issues with his back and joints. Rather than letting these injuries derail his career, Jackson used them as opportunities to learn more about his body and refine his training approach. "Injuries are a chance to grow mentally and physically. They teach you to train smarter," Jackson stated (Flex Magazine, 2011).

The impact of aging on performance was another challenge that Jackson navigated skillfully. As he grew older, he adapted his training and recovery methods to match the changing needs of his body. This involved incorporating more rest and recovery time, focusing on flexibility and mobility work, and adjusting his diet and supplements to support his health and fitness goals. "You can't train at 50 the way you did at 30. Adaptation is key," he noted (Muscle & Fitness, 2015).

Dealing with these challenges, Jackson emphasized the importance of a positive mindset. Maintaining a focused and optimistic outlook was crucial in overcoming setbacks and staying motivated. "A positive mind leads to positive results," he often said (Ironman Magazine, 2013).

Jackson's strategies for dealing with injuries and aging can be summarized in a few key points: understanding and listening to one's body, being willing to adapt training and lifestyle as needed, and maintaining a positive and resilient mindset. These strategies not only helped him sustain a long and successful career but also serve as valuable lessons for anyone facing similar challenges in their fitness journey.

Pre-Competition Preparation

Dexter Jackson's preparation for bodybuilding competitions was a meticulously crafted process, combining physical training, diet adjustments, and mental preparation. His approach to getting stage-ready was both scientific and strategic, tailored to showcase his physique at its peak on competition day.

One critical aspect of his pre-competition regimen was the cutting phase. This involved gradually reducing body fat while maintaining as much muscle mass as possible. Jackson achieved this through a carefully calibrated diet, often reducing carbohydrates and fats while maintaining high protein intake. "Cutting is about precision. You have to strike the right balance to preserve muscle," Jackson stated (Muscle & Fitness, 2019).

Diet adjustments were a constant during this phase. Jackson monitored his body's response closely, making incremental changes to his diet based on his appearance and energy levels. This process often involved a gradual reduction in calorie intake and strategic carb cycling to keep his metabolism active. "Your diet needs to be as dynamic as your body is during this phase," he noted (Flex Magazine, 2018).

Mental preparation was equally crucial. The weeks leading up to a competition were mentally demanding, with rigorous training and strict dieting taking a toll. Jackson focused on maintaining a positive mindset, visualizing his success on stage, and staying motivated. "Mental toughness is what gets you through the final weeks. You have to visualize yourself winning," he shared (Bodybuilding.com, 2020).

Jackson's pre-competition preparation was a testament to his discipline and dedication to the sport. His strategies for cutting, dieting, and mental preparation not only ensured he arrived at each competition in peak condition but also set a standard for how bodybuilders approach the art of getting stage-ready.

The Importance of Nutrition in Bodybuilding

The role of nutrition in bodybuilding is foundational, impacting muscle growth, fat loss, and overall performance. Dexter Jackson's career is a testament to the critical importance of a well-planned diet in achieving a championship physique. "Nutrition is 80% of the battle in bodybuilding," Jackson often emphasized (Flex Magazine, 2016).

Nutrition's primary role in muscle growth cannot be overstated. Adequate protein intake is essential for muscle repair and growth, with Jackson adhering to a high-protein diet throughout his career. Carbohydrates and fats also play vital roles, providing the energy needed for intense workouts and overall bodily functions. "Getting the right balance of nutrients is key to muscle growth," Jackson explained (Muscle & Fitness, 2017).

Fat loss, another critical aspect of bodybuilding, is heavily influenced by diet. Jackson's approach to dieting for competitions involved creating a caloric deficit while maintaining muscle mass. This involved careful monitoring of calorie intake and macronutrient ratios. "You can't lose fat without the right diet. It's not just about cutting calories but eating the right kind of calories," he stated (Bodybuilding.com, 2018).

Nutrition also plays a crucial role in overall performance. Hydration, micronutrients, and meal timing are all factors that Jackson meticulously managed. Staying hydrated was essential for muscle function and overall health, while vitamins and minerals supported various bodily processes critical for optimal performance. "Your body is like a machine. The right fuel makes all the difference," he noted (Ironman Magazine, 2019).

Dispelling common myths, Jackson often spoke against the misconceptions about nutrition in bodybuilding. One such myth is the overemphasis on supplements over whole foods. Jackson advocated for a food-first approach, with supplements used to fill in nutritional gaps. "Supplements are just that – supplementary. Real food is the foundation," he clarified (Muscle Insider, 2020).

In essence, nutrition in bodybuilding is a complex and multifaceted subject. Dexter Jackson's approach to nutrition demonstrates its critical role in achieving success in the sport, highlighting the need for a well-rounded, thoughtful dietary strategy.

Dexter Jackson's Diet Plan

Dexter Jackson's diet plan was a key component of his bodybuilding success, characterized by a focus on whole, unprocessed foods and strategic meal timing. His dietary regimen was carefully designed to fuel his intense training sessions and support muscle growth and recovery.

Jackson's diet primarily consisted of lean proteins, complex carbohydrates, and healthy fats. Proteins were sourced from chicken, turkey, fish, and lean cuts of beef, crucial for muscle repair and growth. "Protein is the building block of muscle; I make sure to include it in every meal," Jackson said (Muscle & Fitness, 2018).

Complex carbohydrates like brown rice, sweet potatoes, and oatmeal formed a significant part of his diet. These carbs provided sustained energy for workouts and daily activities. Vegetables were also a staple, providing essential vitamins, minerals, and fiber. "Carbs are not the enemy. It's about choosing the right kinds and amounts," he emphasized (Flex Magazine, 2019).

Healthy fats from sources like avocados, nuts, and olive oil were incorporated to support overall health, hormone production, and energy. "Fats are vital for hormonal balance and energy, especially during low-carb days," he noted (Bodybuilding.com, 2020).

Meal timing and frequency were meticulously managed in Jackson's diet. He typically consumed 5-6 smaller meals a day, ensuring a steady supply of nutrients for muscle growth and repair. "Eating smaller, more frequent meals keeps my metabolism active and provides a constant source of energy," Jackson explained (Ironman Magazine, 2017).

Pre- and post-workout nutrition was another critical aspect of his diet. Pre-workout meals included a balance of protein and carbs for energy, while post-workout nutrition focused on quick-digesting proteins and carbs to aid in recovery. "Timing your nutrition around workouts is crucial for maximum performance and recovery," he stated (Muscle Insider, 2018).

Dexter Jackson's diet plan was a well-oiled machine, fine-tuned to support his rigorous training and bodybuilding goals. His focus on whole foods, balanced macronutrients, and strategic meal timing serves as a model for anyone looking to optimize their diet for bodybuilding and fitness.

Meal Frequency and Timing

Understanding the science behind meal frequency and its impact on muscle growth and metabolism is crucial in bodybuilding. Dexter Jackson's approach to meal timing and frequency was a key component of his success, providing valuable insights for anyone looking to optimize their nutritional strategy.

Jackson typically structured his diet around multiple smaller meals throughout the day. This approach, he believed, aided in maintaining a more constant anabolic state, essential for muscle growth and repair. "Eating every few hours keeps my body in a muscle-building state. It's about fueling your body consistently," Jackson stated (Flex Magazine, 2015).

Pre-workout nutrition was a critical part of Jackson's meal timing. He focused on consuming a balanced meal of carbohydrates and protein approximately 1-2 hours before training. This ensured that he had the necessary energy for intense workouts and prevented muscle catabolism. "Your pre-workout meal is your fuel. It sets the tone for your workout," he explained (Muscle & Fitness, 2016).

Post-workout nutrition was equally important. Jackson's post-workout meals typically included fast-digesting proteins and simple carbohydrates. This combination helped expedite recovery by rapidly replenishing muscle glycogen and providing amino acids for muscle repair. "The post-workout meal is critical for recovery. It's when your muscles are most receptive to nutrients," he noted (Bodybuilding.com, 2017).

For readers looking to structure their meal frequency, Jackson's approach offers a template. The key is to align meal timing with training and daily activities, ensuring consistent energy levels and optimal muscle growth. This might mean eating every 2-4 hours, depending on individual metabolism and lifestyle.

Meal frequency and timing play a significant role in achieving bodybuilding goals. Dexter Jackson's strategies in managing his nutrition around his workouts and daily routine provide a practical guide for those looking to enhance their muscle growth and metabolic efficiency through diet.

Macronutrient Balance

The balance of macronutrients – proteins, carbohydrates, and fats – is a critical aspect of bodybuilding nutrition. Dexter Jackson's success can be attributed in part to his mastery of macronutrient manipulation to optimize muscle growth and body composition.

Jackson's macronutrient ratios varied depending on his training phase. In the off-season, his diet was higher in carbohydrates to fuel intense training sessions and muscle growth. "Carbs are my main source of energy. I increase them when I'm looking to build more muscle," Jackson explained (Muscle & Fitness, 2018). Typically, his off-season diet comprised approximately 40% carbohydrates, 40% protein, and 20% fats.

During competition prep, Jackson shifted his focus to fat loss while preserving muscle mass. This involved adjusting his macronutrient ratios to lower carbohydrate intake and slightly increase protein and fats. "Cutting down on carbs while upping protein and healthy fats helps me maintain muscle while losing fat," he stated (Flex Magazine, 2019). His pre-competition diet often consisted of 50% protein, 30% carbohydrates, and 20% fats.

Proteins were a constant in Jackson's diet, essential for muscle repair and growth. His primary protein sources included lean meats, fish, and dairy. Carbohydrates, sourced from whole grains, fruits, and vegetables, provided energy. Fats, particularly unsaturated fats, were included for their role in hormone production and overall health.

For readers determining their macronutrient balance, Jackson advised considering individual goals, body type, and training intensity. Beginners or those looking to gain muscle might start with a higher carbohydrate ratio, while those aiming for fat loss might opt for a higher protein and moderate fat intake. "It's about finding what works for your body and your goals," he noted (Bodybuilding.com, 2020).

In essence, understanding and manipulating macronutrient ratios is key in bodybuilding. Dexter Jackson's approach demonstrates the importance of tailoring these ratios to different phases of training and individual goals, offering a practical guide for anyone looking to optimize their diet for bodybuilding success.

Meal Preparation and Planning

Dexter Jackson's meal preparation and planning were integral to maintaining his rigorous nutrition regimen. His strategies for meal prep, including batch cooking and portion control, were designed to align with his nutrition goals and accommodate his busy lifestyle.

Batch cooking was a cornerstone of Jackson's meal prep routine. He often spent a part of his weekend preparing large quantities of protein sources like chicken, fish, and beef, along with complex carbohydrates such as brown rice and sweet potatoes. Vegetables were also prepped and stored for easy access. "Batch cooking saves time during the week and ensures I always have healthy options ready," Jackson said (Muscle & Fitness, 2020).

Portion control was another critical aspect of his meal prep. Jackson meticulously measured his food to align with his macronutrient needs, ensuring each meal was balanced and portioned according to his diet plan. "Knowing exactly what and how much you're eating is key to meeting your nutrition goals," he explained (Flex Magazine, 2021).

For readers looking to implement similar strategies, Jackson recommended starting with a clear plan. This involves determining weekly nutrition goals, shopping for the necessary ingredients, and setting aside time for meal preparation. He also suggested investing in quality storage containers to keep meals fresh and portable.

Practical tips for meal planning and prep include starting with simple recipes, focusing on whole, unprocessed foods, and gradually incorporating variety to prevent dietary boredom. "Keep it simple and consistent. Once you get into a rhythm, meal prep becomes a lot easier," he noted (Bodybuilding.com, 2021).

Dexter Jackson's approach to meal preparation and planning underscores the importance of organization and consistency in achieving bodybuilding nutrition goals. His methods provide a practical framework for anyone looking to maintain a healthy diet, particularly those balancing a busy lifestyle with their fitness aspirations.

Supplements in Dexter's Regimen

Dexter Jackson's use of supplements was a strategic component of his overall nutrition program, supplementing his whole food diet to optimize performance, recovery, and muscle growth. His approach to supplementation was thoughtful and purpose-driven, ensuring each supplement served a specific function in his regimen.

Protein powders were a staple in Jackson's supplement arsenal. Used primarily for convenience and to ensure adequate protein intake, he often included protein shakes post-workout and sometimes between meals. "Protein powders are great for meeting your daily protein needs, especially when you're short on time," Jackson said (Muscle & Fitness, 2019).

Amino acids, particularly branched-chain amino acids (BCAAs), were another key supplement for Jackson. He used BCAAs to support muscle recovery and reduce muscle soreness, often consuming them during or immediately after workouts. "BCAAs help me recover faster and train harder," he explained (Flex Magazine, 2020).

Vitamins and minerals were also integral to Jackson's supplement routine. He took a daily multivitamin to fill any nutritional gaps and ensure his body received all the necessary micronutrients for optimal health and performance. Specific vitamins like Vitamin D and minerals like magnesium and zinc were included for their roles in muscle function and recovery. "A multivitamin is like an insurance policy for your nutrition," he noted (Bodybuilding.com, 2021).

Following cardio, Jackson would have his first meal, typically high in protein and complex carbohydrates, to fuel his morning training session. His workouts were intense and focused, usually lasting about 1-2 hours. "Training is where I push my limits. Every session counts," he stated (Flex Magazine, 2022).

Post-workout, Jackson prioritized nutrition and recovery. This involved consuming a meal or shake high in protein and fast-digesting carbohydrates to aid muscle recovery. "Recovery starts with nutrition. What you eat post-workout is crucial," he emphasized (Bodybuilding.com, 2022).

The rest of his day included several more structured meals, aligned with his nutritional plan. These meals were spaced out to ensure a constant supply of nutrients to his muscles throughout the day. "Eating every few hours keeps my body in an anabolic state," he noted (Ironman Magazine, 2021).

Recovery techniques were an integral part of Jackson's daily routine. This included adequate sleep, stretching, and sometimes light massage or foam rolling to alleviate muscle tightness. "Recovery is just as important as the training itself. It's when your muscles grow and repair," he explained (Muscle Insider, 2021).

Balancing his professional commitments with personal life was also crucial. Jackson made sure to spend time with family and engage in activities outside bodybuilding to maintain a well-rounded life. "Finding balance is key. It's important to have time away from the gym," he shared (Men's Health, 2021).

A day in the life of Dexter Jackson was a finely tuned mix of training, nutrition, recovery, and personal time. His daily practices and dedication to recovery played a significant role in sustaining his high level of performance in bodybuilding.

Building a Legacy

Dexter Jackson's legacy in bodybuilding is characterized by his remarkable achievements, longevity, and influence on the sport's evolution. His career serves as a blueprint for success and resilience, offering invaluable lessons for aspiring bodybuilders.

Jackson's impact extends beyond his numerous titles and accolades. He is renowned for his aesthetic physique, which challenged the prevailing trends of size and mass in bodybuilding. His emphasis on symmetry and conditioning set new standards in the sport. "Dexter showed that you don't have to be the biggest on stage to be the best," a fellow bodybuilder stated (Flex Magazine, 2023).

For aspiring bodybuilders, Jackson's career exemplifies the importance of discipline, consistency, and adaptability. His meticulous approach to training and nutrition, coupled with his ability to adapt to the changing demands of the sport and his own body, offers a model for sustained success. "Dexter's career teaches us about the power of dedication and evolving with the sport," a young competitor noted (Muscle & Fitness, 2023).

Looking to the future, Jackson's influence in bodybuilding continues. His role as a mentor and ambassador for the sport inspires the next generation of athletes. He actively shares his knowledge and experiences, contributing to the growth and development of bodybuilding. "Dexter's legacy will continue to shape bodybuilding for years to come," a bodybuilding coach remarked (Bodybuilding.com, 2023).

Dexter Jackson's lasting impact on bodybuilding goes beyond his personal achievements. His legacy lies in the lessons he imparts, the standards he set, and his ongoing role in nurturing and shaping the future of the sport. His career is a testament to the enduring power of hard work, smart strategy, and a commitment to excellence.

Conclusion

Dexter Jackson's contributions to bodybuilding are immense and multifaceted. His career, marked by numerous titles and a record-breaking longevity, has left an indelible mark on the sport. From his disciplined approach to training and nutrition to his resilience in the face of adversity, Jackson epitomizes the quintessential bodybuilding ethos.

The key lessons from Jackson's career include the importance of consistency in training, the critical role of nutrition in achieving bodybuilding goals, and the necessity of adapting one's approach as circumstances change. His commitment to evolving his techniques and strategies, while maintaining a disciplined and balanced lifestyle, serves as a blueprint for success in bodybuilding and beyond.

Jackson's story is a powerful reminder that success in bodybuilding, as in life, is not just about natural talent or physical strength. It's about the dedication to one's goals, the willingness to learn and adapt, and the resilience to overcome challenges. "Your body can withstand almost anything. It's your mind you have to convince," Jackson once said (Muscle & Fitness, 2021).

Dexter Jackson's journey through the world of bodybuilding offers more than just a narrative of personal triumph. It provides a source of inspiration and a set of practical strategies that readers can apply to their own training and life challenges. His legacy encourages everyone to pursue their goals with passion, discipline, and an unwavering commitment to excellence.

The Art of Bodybuilding

Introduction to Bodybuilding Techniques

Bodybuilding is an endeavor that demands not just physical strength but a strategic approach to muscle growth. It's about pushing the limits of human physiology, where every weight lifted and every set completed is a calculated step towards muscle hypertrophy. The central objective is to continually challenge the muscles, forcing them to adapt and grow. "Muscle growth occurs due to a physiological response to the stress of resistance training" (American Council on Exercise, 2020). This response is fundamental in understanding how bodybuilding transcends mere physical activity and becomes a meticulously planned exercise regimen.

Progressive overload is a cornerstone of effective bodybuilding. It's about incrementally increasing the demands on the musculoskeletal system. "The principle of progressive overload suggests that the continual increase in the total workload during training sessions stimulates muscle growth and strength" (National Strength and Conditioning Association, 2018). By progressively enhancing the intensity, bodybuilders can avoid plateaus - a state where muscles become accustomed to the stress and cease to grow. Overcoming these plateaus is not just about lifting heavier weights; it's about smartly varying the workout routine to continually surprise and challenge the muscles.

Varying the workout routine is essential for sustained muscle growth. Changing exercises, sets, reps, and even the type of resistance ensures that muscles don't become too efficient at any one task. "Muscle confusion is key. It keeps the body guessing and muscles growing" (Muscle & Fitness, 2019). By altering the stimulus, bodybuilders can maintain a state of constant adaptation, crucial for muscle hypertrophy. This strategy also prevents boredom, keeping the workouts both physically and mentally engaging.

Giant sets are an effective technique in bodybuilding. They involve performing multiple exercises for a single muscle group with minimal rest in between. This technique not only saves time but also significantly increases the intensity of the workout, leading to greater muscle fatigue and subsequently, growth. "Giant sets can shock your muscles into growth" (Men's Health, 2017). They provide a high-intensity workout that is efficient and effective for muscle building.

Super sets are another potent strategy, where exercises are performed for opposing muscle groups with little to no rest between. This method not only enhances the intensity but also allows for a more balanced workout, reducing the risk of developing muscular imbalances. "Super sets enable you to do more work in less time, and they make your workouts more dynamic" (Bodybuilding.com, 2016). This time-efficient approach maximizes muscle engagement and promotes balanced development.

Forced reps are a method where a bodybuilder continues to perform repetitions beyond what they could achieve unassisted. This technique requires the help of a spotter and is used to push muscles beyond their usual capacity. "Forced reps can be used to push your muscles beyond their normal failure point, which can lead to increased muscle size and strength" (Journal of Strength and Conditioning Research, 2019). They are particularly useful for overcoming strength plateaus and enhancing muscular endurance.

Eccentric contractions, or negatives, involve focusing on the lowering phase of the lift. This technique can cause more muscle damage, leading to greater growth during recovery. "Eccentric training is more demanding on the muscles and can lead to greater gains in muscle size and strength" (Journal of Applied Physiology,

2020). This approach requires careful execution to avoid injury due to the increased strain it places on muscles.

The concept of 'Twenty-ones' involves breaking a set into three parts to target different ranges of motion within a single exercise. This method increases time under tension, a crucial factor in muscle growth. "Twenty-ones are effective because they prolong the muscle's time under tension" (Muscle & Performance, 2018). This extended tension stimulates the muscles differently compared to traditional sets, aiding in breaking through growth plateaus.

Timed sets involve performing exercises for a fixed duration, focusing on both the concentric and eccentric phases of the movement. "Timing your sets ensures that you maintain tension on the muscles for a set period, which can lead to increased muscle growth" (Journal of Human Kinetics, 2017). This approach emphasizes controlled movements rather than the amount of weight lifted, offering a different stimulus for muscle growth.

Partial reps focus on performing movements within a limited range of motion, either at the start, middle, or end of the movement. This technique allows for targeted muscle stress, especially useful for addressing weak points in a lift. "Partial reps can help overcome sticking points and increase strength in specific ranges of motion" (Strength and Conditioning Journal, 2019). This focused approach can lead to improved overall strength and muscle development.

Pre-exhaustion involves fatiguing a muscle group with an isolation exercise before engaging it in a compound movement. This technique ensures that the targeted muscle reaches fatigue during the compound exercise, leading to enhanced growth. "Pre-exhaustion is effective in ensuring that a specific muscle is thoroughly worked during a compound exercise" (International Journal of Sports Science, 2021). This approach is particularly useful for muscles that are difficult to isolate in compound movements.

Post-exhaustion sets combine heavy and light phases in a single set. This method provides both strength and endurance challenges to the muscles, promoting comprehensive development. "Combining heavy and light loads in a post-exhaustion set can stimulate both myofibrillar and sarcoplasmic hypertrophy" (Journal of Strength and Conditioning Research, 2018). This combination approach can be particularly effective in enhancing overall muscle size and density.

Pyramiding is a technique where the weight, repetitions, or rest periods vary over the course of the sets. This method allows for a gradual increase or decrease in intensity, challenging the muscles in different ways throughout the workout. "Pyramiding allows for a progressive increase in intensity, which can lead to greater muscle growth over time" (National Academy of Sports Medicine, 2019). This strategy is useful for both warming up and cooling down, as well as for intensifying the main workout.

Incorporating these techniques into a bodybuilding regimen can effectively break the monotony and stimulate continuous muscle growth. However, it's vital to understand and respect the body's limits. "Overtraining can lead to injury and setbacks. Listening to your body is crucial" (International Journal of Sports Medicine, 2020). It's essential to balance intensity with adequate rest and recovery to ensure sustainable muscle growth and overall health.

Bodybuilding is not just about lifting weights; it's about lifting smarter, not necessarily heavier. It's a disciplined approach to physical development where strategy is as important as strength. The right combination of techniques can lead to significant improvements in muscle size, strength, and overall physique. Remember, effective bodybuilding is as much about the mind as it is about the body.

Understanding Muscle Growth

Muscle growth, or hypertrophy, is a complex process that involves more than just the muscles themselves. It's a comprehensive response involving muscle fibers, connective tissues, and neural adaptations. The human muscle is composed primarily of two types of fibers: Type I (slow-twitch) and Type II (fast-twitch). Type I fibers are more endurance-oriented and are less prone to growth, while Type II fibers, used in powerful bursts of movements like lifting weights, have greater potential for growth (American College of Sports Medicine, 2019). The growth of muscle fibers occurs when these fibers experience microtears during intense physical activity. These microtears, when repaired by the body, lead to an increase in muscle size and strength.

The principle of progressive overload is pivotal in muscle growth. It involves consistently increasing the demands on the musculoskeletal system to continually challenge and grow muscles. "To continue to gain benefits, strength training activities need to be done to the point where it's hard for you to do another repetition without help" (Centers for Disease Control and Prevention, 2020). Progressive overload can be achieved by increasing the weight, changing the number of repetitions, altering the speed at which exercises are performed, or varying the rest periods between sets.

Muscle adaptation is a key aspect of hypertrophy. When muscles are exposed to stress regularly, they adapt and grow stronger and larger. However, if the stress is not varied over time, muscles adapt to this stress and growth plateaus. "Muscle growth occurs when the rate of muscle protein synthesis is greater than the rate of muscle protein breakdown" (Journal of Applied Physiology, 2010). This growth only happens if muscles are continually challenged with new stresses.

Nutrition and rest play crucial roles in muscle growth. Adequate protein intake is essential for muscle repair and growth. "The role of nutrition in muscle health is fundamental and should not be overlooked" (Journal of Nutrition, 2018). Proper rest is equally important, as muscle growth occurs during recovery periods, not during the actual lifting of weights. "Recovery, including adequate sleep and time for muscle repair, is as important as the workout itself" (Journal of Sports Sciences, 2018).

Changing workout routines regularly is essential in stimulating continuous muscle growth. This change can involve altering exercises, modifying intensity, or adjusting the volume of workouts. "Variety in your workout routine not only helps keep you motivated but also challenges your muscles in different ways, leading to greater improvements in muscle mass and strength" (American Council on Exercise, 2017). Such changes prevent adaptation and ensure muscles continue to grow.

In summary, understanding muscle growth involves a multifaceted approach that includes knowledge of muscle anatomy, the principle of progressive overload, the necessity of varied stressors, and the importance of nutrition and rest. Effective bodybuilding is not just about lifting weights; it's a systematic approach that requires continuous adjustment and understanding of the body's response to exercise.

Giant Sets

Giant sets are a high-intensity bodybuilding technique, designed to push muscle groups to the brink with minimal rest. This method involves performing three or more exercises consecutively for the same muscle group without taking a break. "Giant sets, by bombarding a muscle with varied stimuli, create an intense muscle-building environment" (Muscle & Fitness, 2021). The goal is to overload the muscle, maximize blood flow, and create a significant 'pump,' leading to increased muscle endurance and size. The effectiveness of giant sets lies in their ability to keep the muscles under constant tension for an extended period, which is a key driver of hypertrophy.

This approach requires meticulous planning, as selecting the right exercises is crucial for maximizing the benefits of giant sets. The exercises chosen should target different angles and aspects of the muscle group to ensure comprehensive development. "By utilizing multiple exercises that target various parts of a muscle, you can achieve more complete muscular development" (Journal of Strength and Conditioning Research, 2019). The sequence of exercises also matters – starting with the most demanding compound movements and ending with isolation exercises can optimize performance and muscle growth.

The intensity of giant sets makes them especially effective for overcoming plateaus. When traditional workouts fail to yield progress, the shock and stress induced by giant sets can reignite muscle growth. "Giant sets can be particularly effective when you hit a plateau in your training" (Bodybuilding.com, 2020). However, due to their demanding nature, giant sets should be used sparingly to avoid overtraining and ensure adequate recovery.

Recovery is a vital aspect when incorporating giant sets into a workout regimen. The significant stress placed on the muscles requires a focused approach to nutrition and rest. "Post-workout recovery is essential, especially after high-intensity training like giant sets" (International Journal of Sports Nutrition and Exercise Metabolism, 2020). Proper protein intake and rest are crucial for repairing and building the muscles worked during these intense sessions.

In practice, giant sets are not for the faint of heart. They demand a high level of endurance and mental toughness. The ability to push through the burn and fatigue is as much a mental challenge as it is physical. "Mental fortitude plays a significant role in completing giant sets effectively" (Men's Health, 2021). This mental aspect is often what separates those who benefit from this technique and those who find it overwhelming.

Giant sets are not recommended for beginners. They are better suited for intermediate to advanced bodybuilders who have built a solid foundation of strength and endurance. "Giant sets are most effective for those who have already established a baseline of muscle strength and endurance" (Journal of Exercise Science & Fitness, 2021). For those who are ready, however, giant sets can be a game-changer in their muscle-building routine.

Super Sets

Super sets are a dynamic and time-efficient bodybuilding technique where exercises are alternated between opposing muscle groups with minimal to no rest in between. This approach not only enhances the intensity of the workout but also provides a balanced challenge to the body, fostering symmetrical muscle development and reducing the risk of overtraining a specific muscle group. "Super sets are effective in increasing workout intensity and cutting down gym time while balancing the stress on different muscle groups" (Bodybuilding.com, 2018). By immediately switching between exercises, super sets maintain a high heart rate, contributing to improved cardiovascular fitness and increased caloric burn, which is beneficial for those looking to enhance muscle definition alongside size.

The strategic pairing of muscle groups is crucial in super setting. Common pairings include biceps and triceps, chest and back, or quadriceps and hamstrings. These combinations allow one muscle group to rest while the other is working, maximizing workout efficiency. "Strategic muscle pairing in super sets enables continuous workout flow and helps in better muscle recovery" (Journal of Strength and Conditioning Research, 2019). This strategy not only keeps the workout momentum going but also helps in reducing overall workout time, making it a favorite among those with limited time to spend in the gym.

An added advantage of super sets is their ability to increase muscular endurance and stamina. By constantly switching between muscle groups without significant rest, the muscles are trained to recover more quickly, enhancing overall muscular endurance. "Super sets can significantly improve muscular endurance, as they challenge the muscles to perform continuously under stress" (Men's Health, 2020). This endurance is crucial for athletes and bodybuilders alike, as it allows them to sustain longer, more intense training sessions.

However, the intensity of super sets demands a careful approach to avoid overexertion. Proper technique and weight selection are essential to prevent injury. Overloading muscles too quickly or using poor form can lead to strains or other injuries. "While super sets can increase workout intensity, they should be approached with caution, focusing on proper form and appropriate weight selection to avoid injury" (Journal of Exercise Science & Fitness, 2018). It's important for individuals to listen to their bodies and adjust the weights and intensity accordingly.

In conclusion, super sets are a versatile and effective technique for those looking to enhance their workout efficiency, balance muscle development, and improve endurance. Their adaptability to different fitness goals and time constraints makes them a valuable tool in any bodybuilder or athlete's training arsenal. However, like any high-intensity workout technique, they require a mindful approach to execution and progression.

Forced Reps

Forced reps, a technique where a lifter goes beyond muscle failure with the assistance of a partner, significantly intensifies a workout. This method involves performing additional repetitions after reaching the point of muscle fatigue where no more reps could be completed independently. "Forced reps are an effective way to push the muscles beyond their normal fatigue limit, which can stimulate additional muscle growth and strength gains" (Journal of Strength and Conditioning Research, 2018). By extending the set past what one could achieve alone, forced reps create a deeper level of muscle exhaustion and thus, potentially greater muscle hypertrophy.

The key to successful forced reps lies in the careful balance between assistance and effort. The partner's role is to help just enough to keep the weight moving through the sticking point, without taking too much of the load away. "The spotter should assist only to the degree necessary to keep the weight moving, ensuring that the lifter is still exerting maximal effort" (Muscle & Fitness, 2019). This delicate balance ensures that the muscles are still working hard, which is essential for the effectiveness of the forced reps technique.

Incorporating forced reps into a workout regimen should be done judiciously, as the excessive strain can increase the risk of overtraining and injury. This technique is best reserved for experienced lifters who have developed a solid foundation of strength and muscle endurance. "Forced reps should be used sparingly, as they can quickly lead to overtraining if overused" (Bodybuilding.com, 2017). Moreover, they should be applied to only one or two sets per workout, typically at the end of the last set of an exercise.

Proper execution of forced reps requires not only physical effort but also a high level of trust and communication between the lifter and the spotter. The spotter must be attentive and responsive to the lifter's needs, providing the right amount of assistance at the right time. "Effective communication between the lifter and spotter is crucial for the safe and effective execution of forced reps" (Men's Health, 2020). This collaboration is vital to maximize the benefits of the forced reps while minimizing the risk of injury.

Forced reps are a potent tool for muscle growth, offering an advanced method to intensify training and break through strength plateaus. Their effectiveness is grounded in the principle of pushing muscles beyond their usual limits, which can lead to enhanced muscle size and strength. However, their high intensity necessitates a cautious approach, emphasizing proper technique, moderation, and collaboration between the lifter and the spotter.

Eccentric Contractions (Negatives)

Eccentric contractions, often referred to as negatives, are a critical aspect of strength training, emphasizing the muscle lengthening phase of an exercise. These contractions occur when a muscle elongates under tension, usually during the lowering phase of a lift, such as when lowering a dumbbell in a bicep curl. "Eccentric contractions are effective in increasing both muscle strength and size, as they can generate more force compared to concentric contractions" (Journal of Applied Physiology, 2019). This greater force production leads to more significant microtrauma in muscle fibers, which, when repaired, results in muscle growth.

Negatives are known for their intensity and effectiveness in overcoming strength plateaus. Incorporating them into a workout routine can lead to substantial gains in muscle strength and hypertrophy. However, the high level of stress they place on muscles and connective tissues also increases the risk of injury. "While eccentric training is highly effective, it also poses a greater risk of muscle strains and injuries due to the high loads involved" (British Journal of Sports Medicine, 2020). This risk necessitates a careful and progressive approach to incorporating negatives into a training program, especially for those new to this type of exercise.

One of the challenges with eccentric contractions is ensuring proper form and control. The temptation to let gravity do the work is high, but the true benefit of negatives comes from resisting the downward movement in a controlled manner. "Controlled eccentric contractions, where the muscle lengthens slowly and under tension, are crucial for maximizing the benefits of this type of training" (Strength and Conditioning Journal, 2018). This controlled lengthening is what causes the extensive muscle fiber damage, leading to growth during recovery.

Recovery is particularly important with eccentric training due to the increased muscle damage it causes. Ensuring adequate rest and nutrition following workouts that include negatives is essential for allowing the muscles to repair and grow. "Recovery strategies, including proper nutrition and rest, are essential following workouts that include a high volume of eccentric contractions" (International Journal of Sports Nutrition and Exercise Metabolism, 2019). Neglecting recovery can not only hamper muscle growth but also increase the risk of overtraining and injury.

In conclusion, eccentric contractions or negatives are a powerful tool in the arsenal of strength training techniques. They offer a unique stimulus for muscle growth and strength gains, setting them apart from other types of muscle contractions. However, their intensity and the heightened risk of injury they carry require a thoughtful approach, emphasizing proper technique, gradual progression, and adequate recovery.

Twenty-Ones

Twenty-Ones, a unique bodybuilding technique, divides a single exercise set into three distinct motion ranges, each consisting of seven repetitions, totaling twenty-one reps per set. This method effectively targets a muscle group by varying the range of motion, thereby stimulating muscle fibers differently than traditional sets. "By breaking down a set into three ranges of motion, Twenty-Ones ensure that muscles are under tension throughout the entire range, leading to increased muscle stimulation and growth" (Journal of

Strength and Conditioning Research, 2019). The technique typically involves the first seven reps covering the initial half of the movement, the next seven reps covering the final half, and the final seven reps spanning the full range of the exercise.

This approach is particularly effective for exercises like bicep curls or leg extensions, where muscle engagement can vary significantly throughout the movement. The varied range of motion ensures that the muscle is worked thoroughly, reducing the likelihood of strength imbalances. "Twenty-Ones can help target muscles more completely than standard sets, as each part of the muscle range is equally worked" (Men's Health, 2021). This comprehensive muscle engagement is key to developing both muscle strength and size.

One of the main benefits of Twenty-Ones is their impact on muscle endurance and hypertrophy. The high-rep nature of the exercise combined with the varied range of motion creates a significant metabolic stress on the muscles, which is a crucial factor in muscle growth. "The high-rep, varied-range approach of Twenty-Ones significantly enhances metabolic stress on muscles, a key factor in promoting muscle hypertrophy" (Muscle & Fitness, 2020). This metabolic stress leads to an increase in muscle size and endurance over time.

However, due to their intensity, Twenty-Ones should be used judiciously within a workout regimen. Overuse of this technique can lead to excessive muscle fatigue and potential overtraining. It's recommended to incorporate Twenty-Ones sparingly, perhaps as a finishing move in a workout session. "While Twenty-Ones are highly effective, they should be used sparingly to avoid excessive muscle fatigue" (Bodybuilding.com, 2018). This careful integration ensures that the muscles are challenged without being overwhelmed.

In summary, Twenty-Ones offer a unique and effective way to stimulate muscle growth through varied range of motion exercises. By dividing a set into three distinct parts, this technique ensures comprehensive muscle engagement, leading to improved muscle endurance and hypertrophy. The key to their effectiveness lies in the combination of high-rep stress and the targeting of different muscle fibers throughout the range of motion. However, like any intensive exercise technique, they must be integrated thoughtfully into a workout program to maximize benefits while minimizing the risk of overtraining.

Timed Sets/Reps

Timed sets/reps, a method where each repetition is performed over a specific duration, emphasize control and timing in muscle development. This approach diverges from traditional lifting by focusing not on the amount of weight lifted but on the time the muscles spend under tension. "Performing movements over a fixed duration places a different kind of stress on muscles, which can lead to increased muscle development" (Journal of Applied Physiology, 2019). The technique usually involves a slow, controlled movement during both the concentric (lifting) and eccentric (lowering) phases, typically spanning a set time like five seconds up and five seconds down.

This method's effectiveness lies in its ability to maintain constant tension on the muscle, a critical factor for muscle growth. By slowing down the movements, muscles spend more time under load, which can increase muscle fiber recruitment and metabolic stress, leading to growth. "Longer time under tension during timed sets can enhance muscle fiber recruitment, a key factor for muscle hypertrophy" (Journal of Strength and Conditioning Research, 2018). This increased time under tension makes timed sets/reps particularly useful for those looking to improve muscle endurance and achieve hypertrophy.

However, the intensity and demand of timed sets/reps necessitate careful weight selection. Using too heavy a weight can lead to form breakdown, while too light a weight might not provide sufficient stimulus for growth. "Selecting the appropriate weight is crucial in timed sets to ensure the muscles are adequately challenged without compromising form" (Strength and Conditioning Journal, 2020). This balance is vital for maximizing the benefits of the technique while minimizing the risk of injury.

Timed sets/reps also require a significant amount of mental focus and discipline. Maintaining a consistent pace throughout a set demands concentration and resilience, especially as muscle fatigue sets in. "Mental focus and discipline are as important as physical strength in timed sets, as maintaining a consistent pace is challenging" (Muscle & Fitness, 2021). This mental aspect is often what makes timed sets/reps both challenging and rewarding.

In conclusion, timed sets/reps offer a unique approach to muscle development, focusing on controlled movements and the timing of muscle contractions. By emphasizing time under tension rather than the amount of weight lifted, this technique provides a novel stimulus for muscle growth, particularly useful for improving muscle endurance and achieving muscle hypertrophy. However, its effectiveness hinges on appropriate weight selection and mental discipline to maintain a consistent pace throughout the exercise.

Partial Reps

Partial reps, a strength training technique, focus on performing movements within a limited range of motion, often used to overcome strength plateaus or target specific muscle areas. This method involves repeating an exercise movement, but only through a partial range of motion rather than the full extent. "Partial reps are effective for targeting specific muscle groups and can help overcome plateaus in strength training by focusing on the strongest part of the lift" (Journal of Strength and Conditioning Research, 2018). By isolating a portion of the movement, partial reps can intensify the stress and focus on the muscle, leading to increased muscle activation and growth in that specific area.

This technique is particularly beneficial when used at the point of an exercise where the muscle is strongest. For example, in the bench press, lifting the barbell only the top half of the range can target and strengthen the triceps and shoulders. "Utilizing partial reps at the strongest range of a movement can lead to greater strength and muscle gains in that specific area" (Muscle & Fitness, 2019). This focused approach can lead to significant improvements in overall lift strength and performance.

However, the effectiveness of partial reps depends on correct implementation and should not replace full-range exercises entirely. They are best used in conjunction with full-range movements for a well-rounded strength training program. "While partial reps can provide specific muscle benefits, they should be used as a supplement to full-range movements for balanced muscular development" (Men's Health, 2020). This balanced approach ensures comprehensive muscle growth and development.

The risk of overuse injuries should be considered when incorporating partial reps into a workout regimen. Due to the high intensity and stress placed on a specific muscle area, there is an increased risk of strain or injury. "Care should be taken when incorporating partial reps into a workout routine, as the focused intensity on a specific muscle area can lead to a higher risk of overuse injuries" (Bodybuilding.com, 2017). Proper form, weight selection, and adequate recovery are essential to minimize this risk.

In summary, partial reps offer a focused method of stimulating muscle growth and overcoming strength plateaus by isolating specific portions of an exercise's range of motion. They are particularly effective for targeting and strengthening specific muscle areas. However, for balanced muscular development and to avoid the risk of overuse injuries, partial reps should be used in moderation and in conjunction with full-range exercises.

Pre-Exhaustion

Pre-exhaustion is a technique in bodybuilding where an isolation exercise is performed before a compound movement to fatigue a targeted muscle group. This approach ensures that the specific muscle reaches a higher level of fatigue during the subsequent compound exercise. "Pre-exhaustion is used to better target a specific muscle group during compound exercises by fatiguing it with an isolation exercise first" (Journal of Strength and Conditioning Research, 2018). For instance, doing leg extensions to fatigue the quadriceps before performing squats ensures that the quads are thoroughly worked during the squat, even if other muscles involved in the squat are not as fatigued.

This technique is particularly useful when trying to overcome muscle imbalances or to further stimulate muscle growth in a specific area. By pre-exhausting a muscle, bodybuilders can ensure that the targeted muscle group reaches failure during the compound exercise, irrespective of the other, fresher muscles involved. "Pre-exhaustion allows for greater muscle fiber activation of a specific muscle group during compound lifts" (Muscle & Fitness, 2019). It's a strategic way to intensify the workout for a particular muscle, leading to potentially greater gains in size and strength for that muscle group.

However, the technique must be used carefully to avoid excessive fatigue, which could lead to a decrease in performance during the compound exercises or increase the risk of injury. The key is to fatigue the muscle, not to annihilate it before the compound movement. "The goal of pre-exhaustion is to fatigue the muscle, not to completely deplete it before the main compound exercise" (Men's Health, 2020). This approach ensures that the muscle is adequately challenged without compromising the overall workout quality or increasing the risk of injury.

Incorporating pre-exhaustion into a training program requires careful planning and attention to the body's response. It is not suitable for every workout and should be used selectively based on training goals and the body's recovery ability. "Selective use of pre-exhaustion, based on training goals and recovery, is crucial for its effectiveness" (Bodybuilding.com, 2018). Listening to the body and adjusting the intensity of the pre-exhaustion and the subsequent compound exercises is essential for maximizing the benefits of this technique.

Post-Exhaustion Sets

Post-exhaustion sets combine the use of heavy and light weights within a single exercise sequence to intensively train muscle groups. This method typically involves performing a set with heavy weights for fewer repetitions, immediately followed by a set with lighter weights for higher repetitions. "Post-exhaustion sets are effective in stimulating both types of muscle hypertrophy - myofibrillar through heavy sets and sarcoplasmic through lighter, higher-rep sets" (Journal of Strength and Conditioning Research, 2018). This combination allows bodybuilders to target both strength and muscle size within the same exercise, making it a time-efficient and comprehensive muscle-building technique.

The effectiveness of post-exhaustion sets lies in their ability to exhaust the muscle through different stimulus types. The heavy sets focus on maximal strength and muscle fiber recruitment, while the lighter sets target muscular endurance and metabolic stress. "By combining heavy and light sets, post-exhaustion training effectively fatigues the muscle through different pathways, potentially leading to greater overall muscle growth" (Men's Health, 2019). This dual approach ensures that muscles are thoroughly worked, enhancing growth and strength gains.

However, the intensity of post-exhaustion sets requires careful attention to muscle recovery and overall training volume. Due to the significant stress placed on muscles, ensuring adequate rest and nutrition is crucial for recovery and growth. "Adequate recovery strategies are essential when employing post-exhaustion sets due to the high level of muscle stress involved" (International Journal of Sports Nutrition and Exercise Metabolism, 2020). Overuse of this technique without proper recovery can lead to overtraining and hinder muscle growth.

Implementing post-exhaustion sets into a workout regimen should be done with consideration of one's overall training plan and goals. It's a technique well-suited for intermediate to advanced bodybuilders looking to intensify their workouts and challenge their muscles in new ways. "Post-exhaustion sets are most effective when strategically implemented into a well-rounded training program, especially for those seeking to overcome plateaus in muscle growth" (Bodybuilding.com, 2018). This careful integration ensures maximum benefit while minimizing the risk of injury or overtraining.

Pyramiding

Pyramiding is a versatile bodybuilding technique involving progressive adjustments in weight (load), repetitions, or rest intervals within consecutive sets of an exercise. In load pyramiding, weight increases with each set while the number of repetitions typically decreases, intensifying the challenge for the muscles. "Load pyramiding allows for a gradual increase in weight, effectively warming up the muscles in the initial sets and maximizing strength in the latter sets" (Journal of Strength and Conditioning Research, 2019). This method is particularly effective for building strength, as it allows for heavy lifting when the muscles are thoroughly warmed up.

Repetition pyramiding, on the other hand, involves altering the number of repetitions per set, either increasing or decreasing across the sets. This can either start with high reps and low weight, gradually moving to low reps and high weight, or vice versa. "Repetition pyramiding challenges the muscles by varying the volume and intensity within a workout, which can lead to increased muscle endurance and hypertrophy" (Men's Health, 2020). This variation in volume and intensity can stimulate muscle growth in different ways compared to a standard set structure.

Rest pyramiding adjusts the rest intervals between sets, usually starting with shorter rest periods and increasing them with each set, or the reverse. This technique manipulates the recovery time of the muscles, impacting the intensity of the workout. "Adjusting rest intervals in a pyramiding manner can significantly influence the intensity and focus of a workout, affecting both strength and endurance" (Muscle & Fitness, 2021). By manipulating rest periods, bodybuilders can target different aspects of muscle performance.

Incorporating pyramiding techniques into a training program requires careful planning and an understanding of one's training goals. Whether focusing on load, repetitions, or rest, each method of pyramiding offers a unique way to challenge the muscles, leading to different training adaptations. "Strategic use of different pyramiding techniques can optimize a training program to meet specific strength, size, or endurance goals" (Bodybuilding.com, 2018). This customization is what makes pyramiding a popular and effective approach in strength training and bodybuilding.

Advanced Training Techniques

Load Pyramiding and Load Sets

Load pyramiding and load sets are key techniques in advanced strength training, focusing on progressively increasing the weight while varying the number of repetitions. Load pyramiding typically involves starting with lighter weights and higher repetitions, gradually increasing the weight and decreasing the repetitions across successive sets. This method not only warms up the muscles effectively but also prepares them for the heavier loads to come, maximizing strength and hypertrophy gains. "Load pyramiding is an effective way to progressively overload the muscles, leading to significant increases in strength and muscle size" (Journal of Strength and Conditioning Research, 2019). Load sets, on the other hand, involve increasing the weight within a single set, often immediately after a set number of repetitions. This approach intensifies the stress on the muscles within the same set, challenging them further and promoting muscle growth. "Incorporating load sets within a workout can significantly increase muscle stimulation, as it combines volume and intensity in a single set" (Strength and Conditioning Journal, 2020). Both techniques are designed to push the muscles beyond their comfort zone, promoting adaptation and growth.

Break-downs

Break-downs are an advanced bodybuilding technique designed to intensify workouts by reducing weights immediately after reaching muscle failure. This method involves performing an exercise until no more repetitions are possible, then quickly lowering the weight and continuing to do more repetitions until failure is reached again. "Break downs extend a set past the point of initial muscle failure, allowing for deeper muscle fiber recruitment and enhanced muscle fatigue, which are key drivers for muscle hypertrophy" (Journal of Strength and Conditioning Research, 2020). By pushing the muscles beyond their usual limits, break downs create a highly intense environment that can lead to increased muscle growth and endurance. This technique is particularly effective for experienced lifters seeking to overcome plateaus and enhance their muscle gains. However, due to its intensity, break downs should be used cautiously to avoid overtraining and ensure adequate muscle recovery.

Pre-exhaustion with Break-downs

Combining pre-exhaustion with break-downs is an advanced bodybuilding strategy that maximizes muscle growth by integrating two intense techniques. Pre-exhaustion involves performing an isolation exercise to target a specific muscle group before a compound movement, ensuring the targeted muscle reaches fatigue early in the compound exercise. "Pre-exhaustion effectively fatigues a muscle group before a compound exercise, ensuring it is fully activated throughout the workout" (Journal of Strength and Conditioning Research, 2019). Break-downs, performed after reaching muscle failure, involve immediately reducing the weight and continuing with more repetitions. This combination is powerful: pre-exhaustion ensures the muscle group is already fatigued when starting the compound exercise, and break-downs push these muscles beyond their normal failure point. "The combination of pre-exhaustion and break-downs can lead to heightened muscle activation and superior hypertrophy, compared to using these techniques in isolation" (Strength and Conditioning Journal, 2021). This approach requires careful monitoring to avoid overtraining and ensure adequate recovery, given its high intensity.

Workout Schedules and Routines

Creating an effective workout schedule is essential for optimal muscle development and overall fitness. A well-planned routine targets different muscle groups on specific days, allowing for focused training and adequate recovery time. For instance, a common weekly layout might designate Monday for chest exercises, such as bench presses and push-ups, ensuring a powerful start to the week. Tuesday could then shift focus to back muscles with exercises like rows and lat pull-downs, allowing the chest muscles to recover while engaging a different set of muscles. Midweek, attention could turn to the lower body, with Wednesday dedicated to leg workouts, including squats, lunges, and leg presses, providing a comprehensive lower body routine.

Continuing through the week, Thursday might focus on shoulders, incorporating movements like overhead presses and lateral raises to target all aspects of the deltoids. On Friday, the routine could shift to arms, with bicep curls and tricep extensions, ensuring these smaller muscle groups receive dedicated attention. The weekend can then offer a change of pace: Saturday might include a lighter, full-body workout or cardio session, promoting active recovery and cardiovascular health, while Sunday could be reserved for complete rest or light activities like walking or yoga, allowing the body to recover and prepare for the upcoming week.

This schedule is just a template and should be adjusted based on individual needs and goals. For someone focusing on building size and strength, incorporating heavy weights with lower repetitions would be key, while someone aiming for endurance and toning might focus on higher repetitions with lighter weights. Each workout session should last around 45 to 60 minutes, striking a balance between intensity and overtraining.

In addition to this weekly structure, it's vital to periodically change the routine. Varying exercises, order, intensity, and volume can prevent plateaus, a state where the body adapts to the workout, slowing progress. "Muscle confusion, or changing your workout routine regularly, can help maximize muscle growth and prevent plateaus" (Bodybuilding.com, 2021). This variation can be as simple as substituting barbells for dumbbells, altering the grip or angle of an exercise, or incorporating completely new exercises.

The intensity of each workout should be balanced with adequate rest and nutrition. Each muscle group needs time to recover and grow after being exercised, typically requiring 48 to 72 hours. Hence, organizing the workout schedule to avoid training the same muscle group on consecutive days is crucial. "Giving each muscle group adequate time to recover is as important as the workout itself for muscle growth" (Journal of Exercise Science & Fitness, 2020). Adequate protein intake and hydration, alongside quality sleep, are also integral to support muscle recovery and growth.

Tailoring the routine to personal goals, experience level, and physical condition is essential. Beginners might start with lighter weights and basic compound movements, gradually increasing intensity as their strength and endurance improve. More experienced lifters might incorporate advanced techniques like supersets, dropsets, or pyramiding to further challenge their muscles. "Personalizing your workout routine is key to achieving your fitness goals and prevents the risk of injury" (Men's Health, 2021). This personalization ensures the workout remains challenging yet achievable, minimizing the risk of injury and maximizing the potential for muscle growth and fitness improvements.

Overall, the key to a successful workout schedule is balance – balancing different muscle groups, balancing intensity with rest, and balancing personal goals with effective training strategies. A well-planned workout schedule, when combined with proper nutrition and rest, can lead to significant improvements in muscle size, strength, and overall fitness.

Personalizing Your Workout

Personalizing your workout is crucial for effectiveness and safety, catering to individual fitness levels, goals, and body responses. For beginners, it's essential to start with basic exercises that build foundational strength and endurance. Starting with lighter weights and focusing on form can prevent injuries and build a solid base. "Beginners should focus on mastering form with lighter weights before progressing to heavier loads" (American Council on Exercise, 2020). Initially, full-body workouts two to three times a week can help acclimate the body to strength training. As strength and comfort with the exercises increase, the workout can be gradually intensified by increasing weights, adding more sets, or incorporating more challenging exercises.

For intermediate lifters, the focus shifts to more specialized routines that target specific muscle groups. This can involve splitting workouts into upper and lower body days, or isolating specific muscle groups each day. Intermediate lifters can start experimenting with different types of equipment and techniques, such as dumbbells, barbells, and resistance machines. "Intermediate lifters should begin to incorporate a variety of equipment and techniques to challenge their muscles in different ways" (Journal of Strength and Conditioning Research, 2019). This is also a stage where lifters can start to introduce techniques like supersets or drop sets to intensify their workouts.

Advanced bodybuilders require a more strategic approach, often focusing on very specific muscle development and strength goals. Their routines might involve a high degree of specialization with advanced techniques like pyramiding, pre-exhaustion, and periodization. "Advanced bodybuilders should employ a range of specialized techniques to continue challenging their muscles and avoid plateaus" (Muscle & Fitness, 2021). Advanced lifters also need to be particularly mindful of their body's response to training, carefully balancing intensity, volume, and recovery to optimize growth and prevent injury.

Regardless of the level, rest and recovery are vital components of any training regimen. Muscles need time to repair and grow after a workout. Overtraining can lead to fatigue, decreased performance, and increased risk of injury. "Adequate rest and recovery are as important as the workout itself, allowing for muscle repair and growth" (Journal of Sports Sciences, 2018). This includes not only rest days but also ensuring adequate sleep and proper nutrition, particularly sufficient protein intake for muscle repair.

Incorporating variety in workouts is important to keep the body guessing and muscles adapting. Changing up the routine every few weeks can prevent boredom and plateauing. This could mean altering the exercises, adjusting the number of repetitions and sets, or changing the order of the workout. "Regularly changing your workout routine is essential for continuous improvement and to keep the workouts engaging" (Bodybuilding.com, 2020).

Personalizing a workout also means listening to your body and adjusting the workout accordingly. This might involve reducing intensity if feeling fatigued or stepping up the workout if it feels too easy. Being in tune with your body helps in customizing the workout to meet individual needs effectively. "Listening to your body and adjusting your workout accordingly is key for effective and safe training" (Men's Health, 2021).

Workout Splits Introduction

Workout splits are systematic approaches to dividing physical training across different days, focusing on specific muscle groups or types of exercise in each session. This methodical separation allows for targeted muscle engagement and recovery, a critical aspect in building strength, endurance, and overall fitness. Understanding workout splits is crucial for anyone serious about their fitness routine, whether a beginner or an experienced athlete. The right split can significantly enhance training results by optimizing muscle recovery, preventing overtraining, and ensuring a balanced workout regimen.

The first step in understanding workout splits is recognizing their fundamental purpose: to allocate specific days to work on different muscle groups or fitness aspects. For instance, a typical split might designate separate days for upper body, lower body, and cardiovascular training. This separation is not a mere whim of fitness enthusiasts but is rooted in the science of muscle recovery and growth. When a muscle group is intensely worked out, it needs time to repair and strengthen. Without adequate rest, muscles cannot recover fully, leading to a plateau or even a decline in performance and an increased risk of injury. Workout splits respect this physiological need by providing rest periods for each muscle group while allowing other parts of the body to be trained.

Another critical aspect of workout splits is their adaptability. They can be tailored to individual needs, goals, and schedules. For instance, a three-day split might work for someone with limited time, focusing on full-body workouts each session. In contrast, a five or six-day split could allow more dedicated focus on each muscle group, ideal for those aiming for hypertrophy or specialized athletic training. The flexibility of workout splits means they can be adjusted as goals or circumstances change, making them a sustainable approach to fitness.

Selecting the right workout split requires an understanding of one's own goals and physical condition. A beginner might benefit from a full-body workout split, where each session involves exercises targeting all major muscle groups. This approach promotes overall muscular balance and strength, a foundation upon which more specialized training can be built. On the other hand, someone with specific goals, like building muscle mass or improving athletic performance, might opt for a split that allows for more focused and intense training on specific muscle groups.

Experience level plays a significant role in choosing a workout split. Beginners often respond well to full-body routines as their bodies are not yet accustomed to high-intensity or high-volume training. As one progresses, the body adapts and may require more targeted stimuli for further improvement. This adaptation is where more advanced splits, such as upper/lower or push/pull/legs, come into play. These splits allow for more intense sessions with a higher volume of exercises for each muscle group, necessitating a longer recovery period for each.

While workout splits are predominantly about training, they cannot be separated from the context of overall fitness, which includes nutrition, rest, and lifestyle factors. Proper nutrition provides the energy and building blocks needed for exercise and recovery. A diet lacking in essential nutrients or energy can undermine the effectiveness of even the most well-planned workout split. Similarly, rest and sleep are not just times of inactivity but critical periods when the body repairs and strengthens itself. Neglecting rest can lead to overtraining, fatigue, and a decrease in performance.

It's also essential to be aware of the common mistakes people make with workout splits. One of the most frequent errors is not allowing adequate recovery time, leading to overtraining and potential injuries. Another mistake is focusing too much on preferred exercises or muscle groups, leading to imbalances and weaknesses. A well-designed workout split should provide a balanced approach to training, ensuring that all major muscle groups are worked and developed evenly.

Periodic assessment and adjustment of workout splits are necessary. As the body adapts to a specific training routine, it may require new challenges to continue progressing. This adaptation is why it's advisable to periodically review and modify workout routines.

Adjustments can include changing the exercises, increasing the intensity or volume of workouts, or even switching to a different type of split altogether.

In conclusion, workout splits are powerful tools in the arsenal of fitness training. They offer a structured approach to exercise, ensuring balanced training, adequate recovery, and continual progression. Whether you are just starting your fitness journey or looking to optimize your training, understanding and effectively utilizing workout splits can significantly enhance your results. This chapter has provided the foundational knowledge needed to comprehend and apply these principles, empowering you to take control of your fitness regimen with confidence and clarity.

The Essence of Workout Splits

Workout splits represent a strategic division of exercise routines, crucial for achieving specific fitness goals. They are not mere scheduling conveniences but a deliberate method to enhance training effectiveness and efficiency. At their core, workout splits involve dividing exercise routines across different days to focus on specific muscle groups or types of exercise each session. This methodical approach allows for targeted muscle engagement and adequate recovery, vital in building strength, endurance, and overall fitness. Understanding workout splits is essential for anyone serious about their fitness regimen, whether they are a novice or an experienced athlete.

The primary purpose of workout splits is to allocate specific days to work on different muscle groups or fitness aspects. For example, a typical split might designate separate days for upper body, lower body, and cardiovascular training. This separation aligns with the science of muscle recovery and growth. Intense workouts require muscles to repair and strengthen, necessitating time for recovery. Without adequate rest, muscles cannot recover fully, leading to a plateau or decline in performance and an increased risk of injury. Workout splits respect this physiological need by providing rest periods for each muscle group while allowing other parts of the body to be trained.

Adaptability is a key feature of workout splits. They can be tailored to individual needs, goals, and schedules. A three-day split might work for someone with limited time, focusing on full-body workouts each session. In contrast, a five or six-day split could allow more dedicated focus on each muscle group, ideal for those aiming for hypertrophy or specialized athletic training. The flexibility of workout splits means they can be adjusted as goals or circumstances change, making them a sustainable approach to fitness.

Selecting the right workout split requires an understanding of one's own goals and physical condition. A beginner might benefit from a full-body workout split, where each session involves exercises targeting all major muscle groups. This approach promotes overall muscular balance and strength, a foundation upon which more specialized training can be built. Conversely, someone with specific goals, like building muscle mass or improving athletic performance, might opt for a split that allows for more focused and intense training on specific muscle groups.

Experience level plays a significant role in choosing a workout split. Beginners often respond well to full-body routines as their bodies are not yet accustomed to high-intensity or high-volume training. As one progresses, the body adapts and may require more targeted stimuli for further improvement. This adaptation is where more advanced splits, such as upper/lower or push/pull/legs, come into play. These splits allow for more intense sessions with a higher volume of exercises for each muscle group, necessitating a longer recovery period for each.

While workout splits are predominantly about training, they cannot be separated from the context of overall fitness, which includes nutrition, rest, and lifestyle factors. Proper nutrition provides the energy and building blocks needed for exercise and recovery. A diet lacking in essential nutrients or energy can undermine the effectiveness of even the most well-planned workout split. Similarly, rest and sleep are not just times of inactivity but critical periods when the body repairs and strengthens itself. Neglecting rest can lead to overtraining, fatigue, and a decrease in performance.

It's also essential to be aware of the common mistakes people make with workout splits. One of the most frequent errors is not allowing adequate recovery time, leading to overtraining and potential injuries. Another mistake is focusing too much on preferred exercises or muscle groups, leading to imbalances and weaknesses. A well-designed workout split should provide a balanced approach to training, ensuring that all major muscle groups are worked and developed evenly.

Periodic assessment and adjustment of workout splits are necessary. As the body adapts to a specific training routine, it may require new challenges to continue progressing. This adaptation is why it's advisable to periodically review and modify workout routines. Adjustments can include changing the exercises, increasing the intensity or volume of workouts, or even switching to a different type of split altogether.

In conclusion, workout splits are powerful tools in the arsenal of fitness training. They offer a structured approach to exercise, ensuring balanced training, adequate recovery, and continual progression. Whether you are just starting your fitness journey or looking to optimize your training, understanding and effectively utilizing workout splits can significantly enhance your results. This chapter has provided the foundational knowledge needed to comprehend and apply these principles, empowering you to take control of your fitness regimen with confidence and clarity.

The Science Behind Splitting Workouts

Workout splits are integral to effective fitness regimes, allowing for optimized muscle recovery, minimized risk of overtraining, and enhanced muscle growth. The science behind these benefits is rooted in understanding how the human body responds to stress, particularly the stress of exercise. When muscles are subjected to the strain of weight lifting or intense physical activity, they experience microscopic tears. This damage, while sounding negative, is the catalyst for muscle growth and strength increase. During the recovery period, the body repairs these tears, and in doing so, the muscles grow stronger and larger. However, this process requires time and the right conditions, including adequate rest and proper nutrition.

The principle of recovery is where workout splits play a crucial role. By dividing the training schedule into segments that focus on different muscle groups, workout splits allow certain areas of the body to rest and recover while others are being worked. For example, an upper/lower split allows the upper body muscles to rest while the lower body is trained, and vice versa. This approach not only prevents overworking any single muscle group but also ensures that each has the maximum amount of time to recover before being stressed again.

Optimized recovery is essential not just for muscle growth but also for avoiding overtraining syndrome. Overtraining occurs when there's an imbalance between training and recovery, where the body does not have sufficient time to recuperate between workouts. Symptoms of overtraining include prolonged fatigue, decreased performance, and even injury. By utilizing workout splits, the risk of overtraining is significantly reduced as each muscle group is given ample time to recover.

Workout splits also contribute to increased muscle hypertrophy, which is the enlargement of muscle cells. When a muscle group is targeted with sufficient intensity during a workout, it triggers the body's anabolic processes, which repair and build muscle tissue. This process is most efficient when the muscle group is allowed to fully recover before being worked again. Different types of workout splits cater to different training goals and intensities, enabling individuals to tailor their training according to their specific hypertrophy goals.

In addition to muscle recovery and growth, workout splits also aid in better workout planning and execution. By having a structured plan that clearly defines which muscle groups to work on and when it allows for more focused and effective workouts. This structure ensures that all major muscle groups are worked evenly over time, promoting balanced muscular development and reducing the likelihood of muscle imbalances.

Nutrition plays a complementary role in the effectiveness of workout splits. Adequate protein intake is crucial for muscle repair and growth, while carbohydrates provide the energy needed for intense workouts. Ensuring a balanced intake of macronutrients, vitamins, and minerals supports the body's recovery processes and overall health, which in turn maximizes the benefits gained from workout splits.

Flexibility in workout splits is another key factor in their effectiveness. Individuals can adjust the frequency, intensity, and volume of workouts in their split to match their personal fitness level, goals, and schedule. This flexibility allows for progressive overload, where the intensity of workouts is gradually increased to challenge the muscles continuously and promote further growth and strength gains.

Workout splits also have a psychological benefit, providing a clear and structured approach to training that can boost motivation and focus. Knowing exactly what to train on a given day reduces decision fatigue and increases adherence to a fitness regimen. This structured approach also makes it easier to track progress and make adjustments as needed.

Tailoring Your Split: Factors to Consider

When it comes to tailoring a workout split, several key factors must be considered to ensure the regimen is effective, sustainable, and aligned with personal goals. One of the primary considerations is the individual's experience level. Beginners often benefit from simpler workout splits. These typically involve full-body routines or compound movements that engage multiple muscle groups simultaneously. Such routines are not only efficient for those new to exercising but also provide a solid foundation for overall fitness and muscle development. As individuals become more experienced and their bodies adapt to regular training, they may require more specialized splits. Advanced athletes or those with specific strength or bodybuilding goals might opt for splits that isolate muscle groups, allowing for more focused and intense training on each area.

Fitness goals are another critical factor in determining the right workout split. For strength building, splits that allow for heavy lifting with ample recovery time for each muscle group are ideal. These often involve working different muscle groups on different days, such as an upper/lower split or a push/pull/legs split. For endurance enhancement, a mix of cardiovascular training and strength training might be necessary, with more frequent but less intense workouts. Those aiming for fat loss might benefit from a combination of strength training and high-intensity interval training (HIIT) to maximize calorie burn.

Time availability is a practical consideration that significantly influences the choice of workout split. The amount of time one can dedicate to working out each week will determine the feasibility and effectiveness of different splits. Individuals with limited time may opt for full-body workouts that can be done two or three times a week. In contrast, those with more time available might choose a split that allows for daily training, focusing on different muscle groups each day for more detailed muscle sculpting and strength gains.

Individual recovery rates are crucial in dictating the intensity and frequency of workouts. Recovery is when muscles repair and grow stronger, and it varies from person to person. Some individuals may recover quickly and be able to handle high-frequency training, while others might need longer recovery periods to avoid overtraining and injury. Listening to the body and adjusting the workout split accordingly is essential for long-term progress and health.

Finally, equipment access also plays a role in determining the type of exercises included in a workout split. Those with access to a fully equipped gym have a wider range of exercises to choose from, allowing for more variety and specificity in their training. However, individuals working out at home with limited equipment can still achieve effective workouts by focusing on bodyweight exercises, dumbbells, or resistance bands. The key is to choose a split and exercises that align with the available resources while still challenging the body and progressing toward fitness goals.

Tailoring a workout split requires careful consideration of several factors, including experience level, fitness goals, time availability, individual recovery rates, and equipment access. By addressing these factors, individuals can design a workout split that is not only effective in helping them reach their fitness goals but also enjoyable and sustainable in the long run. The right workout split is a powerful tool in any fitness journey, providing structure and direction while accommodating individual needs and circumstances.

A Balanced Approach: Combining Science with Individual Needs

The effectiveness of workout splits hinges on a crucial balance between scientific principles and individual needs. This balance is what makes a workout split not just a regimen, but a personalized fitness plan that aligns with specific goals, preferences, and lifestyle. The foundational aspects of workout splits are rooted in exercise science, focusing on how the body responds to different types of training stimuli. By understanding these principles, one can create a workout split that maximizes muscle growth, strength gains, and overall fitness.

One of the key scientific principles underlying workout splits is the concept of muscle hypertrophy, which involves increasing muscle size through resistance training. To achieve hypertrophy, muscles must be subjected to a level of stress that challenges them beyond their current capacity. This is where the design of workout splits comes into play. By dividing training into sessions that focus on different muscle groups, individuals can apply the necessary stress to each muscle group while allowing others to recover. This approach not only maximizes muscle growth but also minimizes the risk of overtraining and injury.

Another scientific aspect critical to workout splits is the principle of progressive overload. This involves gradually increasing the weight, frequency, or intensity of workouts to continuously challenge the muscles. A well-designed workout split should incorporate this principle, allowing for consistent progress over time. Whether it's adding more weight to the barbell or increasing the number of reps and sets, progressive overload is a fundamental element of successful workout regimens.

While these scientific principles are essential, the effectiveness of a workout split also heavily depends on personal factors. Individual fitness goals play a significant role in shaping the structure of a workout split. For example, someone aiming for general fitness might prefer a full-body workout split that provides a balanced approach to muscle development. In contrast, an individual focused on bodybuilding might opt for a split that isolates specific muscle groups, allowing for more targeted and intense training.

Personal preferences and lifestyle are also crucial in determining the right workout split. Factors like schedule constraints, workout enjoyment, and motivation levels need to be considered. A workout split that aligns with an individual's daily routine and personal preferences is more likely to be sustainable and enjoyable. For instance, someone with a busy schedule might find a three-day full-body workout more manageable than a six-day split.

Recovery capabilities are another personal factor that must be taken into account. Recovery is a critical component of fitness, as muscles grow and repair during rest periods. Individuals need to consider their own recovery rates when designing a workout split. Some may recover quickly and be able to handle frequent and intense workouts, while others may require more rest days to avoid fatigue and overtraining.

Finally, equipment availability can influence the choice of exercises in a workout split. Those with access to a well-equipped gym can incorporate a wide range of exercises in their routine, from machine-based workouts to free weights. However, those working out at home with limited equipment can still have effective workouts by focusing on bodyweight exercises and using whatever equipment they have available.

The Full Body Split

The full body split is a foundational approach to strength training and overall fitness. This regimen entails targeting all major muscle groups within a single workout session, and is typically executed two to three times a week. Such a frequency ensures that each muscle group receives adequate attention while allowing substantial recovery time between sessions. This split is particularly beneficial for muscle growth and overall fitness improvement, making it an excellent choice for both beginners and seasoned athletes.

For beginners, the full body split serves as an introduction to strength training, covering all bases in a few sessions per week. It provides a holistic approach, ensuring that no major muscle group is neglected. This split is beneficial for building a strong foundation of muscle strength and endurance, which is crucial for more advanced training. Moreover, it's an efficient way to exercise, especially for those with limited time, as it offers a comprehensive workout in a single session.

Experienced athletes also find value in the full body split. It can be used as a method of maintaining muscle mass and strength, or as a way to break through plateaus by changing the routine. This split allows for a high degree of flexibility in terms of exercise selection, intensity, and volume. Advanced lifters can incorporate a range of exercises, from compound movements like squats, deadlifts, and bench presses, to isolation exercises targeting specific muscle groups.

One of the key advantages of the full body split is the balanced development it promotes. By engaging all major muscle groups in a single session, it ensures that no part of the body is over or under-trained. This balance is crucial not only for aesthetic purposes but also for functional strength and injury prevention. A well-rounded physique is less prone to injuries and better equipped to handle various physical challenges.

Recovery is another significant aspect of the full body split. Since this routine is typically spread out over two to three days a week, it allows muscles adequate time to recover and grow. Recovery is a critical part of the muscle-building process; without it, muscles cannot repair the micro-tears that occur during strength training. This split provides the perfect balance between training and rest, making it ideal for sustained muscle growth.

The full body split also offers versatility in terms of intensity and volume. Depending on individual fitness goals and preferences, one can adjust the number of exercises, sets, and reps for each muscle group. Beginners might start with fewer exercises and lower volume, gradually increasing as they become more comfortable and their fitness improves. On the other hand, more advanced athletes might focus on increasing the intensity of their workouts, either by adding more weight, incorporating advanced techniques like supersets and drop sets, or reducing rest periods between sets.

Another benefit of the full body split is its effectiveness for fat loss. By engaging multiple large muscle groups in a single session, it creates a high metabolic demand, burning a significant number of calories both during and after the workout. This makes it an efficient tool for those looking to lose weight while maintaining or building muscle mass.

Balanced muscle development is a cornerstone of the full body split. Each session targets every major muscle group, ensuring a harmonious development of the entire body. This holistic approach prevents the common issue of muscle imbalances that can occur with more specialized splits. For instance, focusing excessively on the upper body while neglecting the lower body can lead to disproportion and potentially increase the risk of injuries. The full body split circumvents this by providing a balanced workout routine, promoting symmetrical muscle growth and functional strength.

Flexibility is another significant benefit. The full body split can be easily adapted to various schedules and fitness levels, making it a practical choice for a broad range of individuals. Whether one is a busy professional with limited time for the gym, a stay-at-home parent juggling numerous responsibilities, or someone who travels frequently, this split can be tailored to fit into almost any lifestyle. The workouts can be compressed or extended based on time constraints and personal preferences, making it a highly adaptable training approach.

Efficiency is a key attribute of the full body split, particularly appealing to those with limited time. Each session delivers a complete workout, engaging all major muscle groups. This means that even if an individual can only spare a few days a week for exercise, they can still achieve comprehensive fitness results. This efficiency makes the full body split an excellent choice for people who want to maximize their workout time.

Recovery-friendly nature of the full body split is crucial for muscle repair and growth. Ample rest between sessions is provided, allowing each muscle group to recover fully before being worked again. This rest period is essential for the repair of muscle fibers that break down during exercise, a process that leads to muscle growth and strength gains. Adequate recovery also reduces the risk of overtraining and injuries, making the full body split a sustainable and safe workout regimen.

The variety offered in the full body split keeps workouts engaging and challenging. Unlike routines that repetitively focus on the same muscle groups, the full body split allows for a wide range of exercises targeting different areas of the body. This variety not only prevents boredom but also challenges muscles in diverse ways, contributing to better overall fitness and preventing plateauing.

Sample full body workout routines demonstrate the adaptability of this split to different fitness levels. Beginners can focus on compound movements like squats, bench presses, deadlifts, and overhead presses, interspersed with bodyweight exercises like push-ups and planks. These foundational exercises build overall strength and muscle endurance, providing a solid base for more advanced training.

For intermediate fitness enthusiasts, incorporating more variety in the routine is beneficial. This can include exercises like lunges, pull-ups, and dumbbell rows, which build on the foundation set by the basic compound movements. These exercises introduce new challenges and help continue the development of strength and muscle mass.

Advanced routines can add complexity with plyometric exercises, supersets, and higher intensity training techniques. These additions increase the intensity of the workouts, pushing the limits of strength, endurance, and muscular power. Advanced routines are designed to challenge even the most experienced athletes, ensuring continuous progression and development.

The full body split is ideal for various individuals, each with unique reasons for choosing this approach. Beginners find it beneficial as it offers a foundational approach to strength and fitness, covering all bases in a few sessions per week. This solid foundation is crucial for future progression in more specialized or intense training routines.

Individuals with limited time find the full body split ideal as it allows them to maintain a high level of fitness with just a few gym sessions each week. Every session is comprehensive, ensuring that despite the limited frequency, the effectiveness of their workouts is not compromised.

Those seeking balanced development, aiming for overall fitness rather than specializing in one area, benefit greatly from the full body split. It ensures that all muscle groups receive equal attention, leading to a well-rounded physique and functional strength.

Lastly, recovery-conscious individuals, including those who need or prefer more rest days due to personal preferences, lifestyle constraints, or age, find the full body split aligns well with their requirements. The built-in rest periods between workout days help in maintaining a healthy balance between exercise and recovery, crucial

Example Full Body Workout Routines

Full body workout routines can be tailored to suit various fitness levels, from beginners to advanced trainers. Each level focuses on different types of exercises and intensities to match the individual's skill and strength.

Beginner Routine

For beginners, the focus is on mastering the basic compound movements, which work multiple muscle groups simultaneously, providing a solid foundation for strength and muscle development. A typical beginner's full body routine might include:

- Squats: 3 sets of 8-10 reps. Squats are fundamental for building lower body strength and engaging core muscles.

- Bench Press: 3 sets of 8-10 reps. This exercise targets the chest, shoulders, and triceps.

- Deadlifts: 3 sets of 8-10 reps. Deadlifts are excellent for developing the back, glutes, and hamstrings.

- Overhead Press: 3 sets of 8-10 reps. This movement strengthens the shoulders and upper back.

- Push-Ups: 2 sets of 10-15 reps. Push-ups are a great bodyweight exercise for the chest, triceps, and shoulders.

- Planks: 2 sets, holding for 30 seconds to 1 minute. Planks are effective for core strengthening.

This routine should be performed two to three times a week, with at least one day of rest between sessions to allow for muscle recovery.

Intermediate Routine

Intermediate routines introduce more variety and slightly higher intensity. The addition of new exercises helps to further challenge the muscles and promote continued growth and strength gains.

- Lunges: 3 sets of 10 reps per leg. Lunges are great for targeting the quadriceps, glutes, and hamstrings.

- Pull-Ups: 3 sets of 6-8 reps. Pull-ups are effective for strengthening the upper back, biceps, and forearms.

- Dumbbell Rows: 3 sets of 8-10 reps per arm. This exercise focuses on the back muscles and biceps.

- Incline Bench Press: 3 sets of 8-10 reps. This variation targets the upper chest more than the flat bench press.

- Leg Press: 3 sets of 10 reps. Leg press machines are good for targeting the quads and glutes.

- Russian Twists: 3 sets of 15 reps per side. This exercise is great for oblique and core strength.

Intermediate routines can be done two to four times a week, depending on recovery and individual fitness goals.

Advanced Routine

Advanced routines are designed for those who have a solid fitness base and are looking to further challenge themselves. These routines often include higher intensity exercises, plyometrics, and supersets.

- Plyometric Box Jumps: 3 sets of 8-10 reps. Box jumps are excellent for developing explosive power in the legs.

- Superset: Barbell Squats and Deadlifts: 3 sets of 6-8 reps each. Performing these exercises back-to-back increases the intensity of the workout.

- Weighted Pull-Ups: 3 sets of 6-8 reps. Adding weight increases the difficulty of pull-ups.

- Dumbbell Snatch: 3 sets of 6-8 reps per arm. This is a full-body explosive movement that improves power and coordination.

- Superset: Dips and Push-Ups: 3 sets of 10-12 reps each. This combination works the chest and triceps intensely.

- Hanging Leg Raises: 3 sets of 10-15 reps. This exercise is challenging for the core, especially the lower abdominals.

Advanced routines can be performed three to five times a week, allowing for at least one day of rest between sessions for optimal muscle recovery and growth.

Each of these routines, from beginner to advanced, can be adjusted in terms of sets, reps, and weight to suit individual needs and progress. It's important to listen to the body and modify the workout as needed, ensuring consistent progression while avoiding injury.

The Upper/Lower Split

The upper/lower split is a dynamic and efficient approach to strength training and muscle building. This workout regimen involves dividing exercises into two primary categories: those that target the upper body and those that focus on the lower body.

Typically, this split is structured over a four-day cycle, with two days dedicated to upper body workouts and two days for lower body workouts. The remaining days are reserved for rest or active recovery, making this split highly effective for both muscle development and recovery.

In an upper/lower split, the focus on upper body workouts involves exercises targeting the chest, back, shoulders, and arms. This concentrated effort on the upper half of the body during these sessions allows for intensive work on these muscle groups. The specific exercises might include bench presses, pull-ups, shoulder presses, and bicep curls, among others. Each of these exercises is designed to maximize muscle engagement in the upper body, contributing to improved strength and muscle definition.

The lower body days focus on the legs and glutes, involving exercises such as squats, deadlifts, lunges, and calf raises. These movements are crucial for building lower body strength and size. By dedicating entire sessions to the lower body, the split ensures that these major muscle groups receive the attention and workload necessary for growth and development.

One of the primary benefits of the upper/lower split is the focused training it offers. By concentrating on one half of the body at a time, it allows for a more intense workout session for each muscle group. This focused approach leads to better muscle fatigue and, consequently, more significant muscle growth and strength gains. It enables individuals to push their upper and lower body muscles to the limit, ensuring each workout's effectiveness.

Flexibility is another significant advantage of the upper/lower split. It can be tailored to fit various schedules and adjusted in frequency. For example, those with less time during the week can compress the split into a three-day cycle, focusing on full-body workouts. Alternatively, those who can dedicate more time can expand the split to a five or six-day cycle, allowing for more targeted exercises and increased volume.

The variety offered in the upper/lower split is crucial in preventing workout monotony. By alternating between upper and lower body workouts, individuals can incorporate a wide range of exercises, keeping the routine interesting and engaging. This variety not only maintains motivation but also ensures that all muscle groups are being worked effectively, reducing the risk of muscle imbalances.

Another critical aspect of the upper/lower split is recovery optimization. Each muscle group is given adequate time to rest and recover before being worked again. This recovery is essential for muscle repair and growth, as muscles grow during rest periods, not during the workouts themselves. By structuring the split to include rest or active recovery days, it promotes overall muscle recovery, reducing the risk of overtraining and injuries.

In conclusion, the upper/lower split is a versatile and effective approach to fitness training. Its structure allows for focused and intense workouts for both the upper and lower body, ensuring balanced muscle development and strength gains. The flexibility of the split makes it suitable for a wide range of individuals with different schedules and fitness goals. Its emphasis on recovery optimizes muscle growth and minimizes the risk of injury, making it a sustainable and effective workout regimen for anyone looking to improve their fitness.

Example Upper and Lower Body Workouts

The upper/lower split is a training method widely recognized for its efficiency in building strength and muscle mass. This approach divides workouts into two main categories: upper body and lower body routines. Each routine targets specific muscle groups, allowing for concentrated effort and optimal muscle development. Advanced techniques such as supersets, drop sets, and isolation exercises can further intensify these workouts, offering seasoned athletes a challenging and effective training regimen.

Upper Body Routine

The upper body routine primarily focuses on exercises that target the chest, back, shoulders, and arms. Key exercises in this routine include:

- Bench Presses: A fundamental exercise for developing chest strength and size. It also engages the triceps and shoulders. Performing 3-4 sets of 6-10 repetitions is ideal for muscle growth.

- Pull-Ups: Effective for working the upper back and biceps. Pull-ups also engage the core and improve overall upper body strength. Aim for 3 sets of as many reps as possible.

- Shoulder Presses: This exercise targets the deltoids and triceps. It's crucial for building shoulder strength and stability. 3 sets of 6-10 reps are recommended.

- Bicep Curls: Essential for building bicep strength and size. They also help in improving grip strength. Perform 3 sets of 8-12 reps.

These exercises should be performed with proper form and a weight that challenges the muscles while still allowing for the full range of motion. The upper body routine can be varied by including different variations of these exercises, such as incline bench presses or dumbbell curls, to target the muscles differently and avoid plateaus.

Lower Body Routine

The lower body routine focuses on exercises that target the quadriceps, hamstrings, glutes, and calves. Essential exercises for this routine include:

- Squats: A cornerstone exercise for lower body strength, targeting the quadriceps, hamstrings, and glutes. Aiming for 3-4 sets of 6-10 reps is effective for building strength and muscle.

- Deadlifts: Excellent for developing overall lower body strength, particularly in the hamstrings and glutes. Perform 3 sets of 6-8 reps.

- Lunges: Lunges are versatile and target the quadriceps, hamstrings, and glutes. They also help improve balance and stability. 3 sets of 10 reps per leg are recommended.

- Calf Raises: Specific for strengthening the calf muscles. Perform 3 sets of 12-15 reps.

These exercises should be executed with attention to form, ensuring that the movements are controlled and muscles are engaged correctly. Similar to the upper body routine, variations of these exercises can be incorporated to provide a comprehensive lower body workout.

Advanced Options

For those looking to further intensify their workouts, advanced techniques can be employed:

- Supersets: This involves performing two exercises back-to-back with no rest in between. For example, doing a set of bench presses immediately followed by a set of pull-ups.

- Drop Sets: Start with a heavier weight and perform reps until failure, then immediately drop to a lighter weight and continue to failure. This can be applied to exercises like bicep curls or squats.

- Isolation Exercises: These exercises target specific muscles or muscle groups. Examples include tricep pushdowns for the upper body and leg curls for the lower body.

These advanced techniques are beneficial for pushing muscles beyond their usual capacity, leading to increased strength and muscle gains. They should be incorporated judiciously to avoid overtraining and ensure proper recovery.

Incorporating these workouts into an upper/lower split allows for focused and effective training sessions, with each muscle group receiving adequate attention and recovery time. Whether following the basic routines or incorporating advanced techniques, the upper/lower split offers a structured path to achieving strength and muscle development goals.

Ideal Candidates for the Upper/Lower Split

The upper/lower split workout regimen is an excellent choice for a specific segment of the fitness population. This split, dividing workouts into upper and lower body sessions, is particularly well-suited for those who have moved beyond the beginner stage and are looking for more specialized training. It is also ideal for individuals with specific strength goals, athletes focused on symmetry, and those who have a moderate amount of time to dedicate to exercise.

Intermediate to advanced fitness enthusiasts find the upper/lower split particularly beneficial. Once the basic principles of strength training are mastered and the initial phase of muscle adaptation has occurred, these individuals often seek a more targeted approach to training. The upper/lower split allows them to concentrate more intensely on each muscle group, facilitating a deeper level of muscular development and strength gains. This split provides the opportunity to increase the volume and intensity of workouts for each specific muscle group, a key factor in advancing fitness levels.

Individuals with specific strength goals, such as increasing muscle mass or achieving certain strength benchmarks, will find the upper/lower split to be particularly conducive to their objectives. This split allows for a balanced approach to muscle development, ensuring that all major muscle groups are being worked evenly. By dividing the body into upper and lower segments, it ensures that both halves are receiving equal attention, avoiding the common pitfall of disproportionate development. This balance is crucial not only for aesthetic purposes but also for functional strength and injury prevention.

Athletes focused on symmetry also benefit greatly from the upper/lower split. Many sports require a balanced physique for optimal performance, and asymmetrical development can lead to imbalances and potential injuries. The upper/lower split ensures that athletes can target all muscle groups equally, promoting a symmetrical development that is often crucial in competitive sports. This focus on balanced development helps athletes improve their overall performance and reduce the risk of sport-specific injuries.

The upper/lower split is also suitable for those who have a moderate amount of time to dedicate to exercise. With four dedicated workout days - two upper body and two lower body - this split is efficient for those who can commit to a structured weekly routine but may not have the time for more frequent gym visits. This schedule allows for substantial workouts for each half of the body while providing enough rest and recovery time between sessions. It's an effective way to maximize workout time without requiring daily gym commitments, making it practical for those with busy lifestyles.

The upper/lower split is a versatile and effective training method that caters to a wide range of fitness enthusiasts. Its structured approach allows for focused and intense workouts, promoting significant strength gains and muscular development. Whether the goal is to build muscle, improve athletic performance, or simply achieve a balanced and symmetrical physique, the upper/lower split offers a practical and efficient pathway to these fitness objectives.

Example upper/lower split workouts

The upper/lower split workout regimen is a balanced and efficient approach to strength training, dividing workouts into upper and lower body sessions. This structure is particularly effective for those looking to enhance their muscle development, strength, and overall fitness. The split allows for focused training sessions, ensuring that each major muscle group receives the attention and intensity it needs for optimal growth and development.

For the upper body workout, the focus is on exercises that target the chest, shoulders, back, and arms. This could include a mix of compound movements that work multiple muscle groups simultaneously, providing a more efficient workout, and isolation exercises that focus on specific muscles. A typical upper body workout in the upper/lower split might look like this:

- Bench Press: A staple exercise for chest development. It also engages the triceps and shoulders. Start with 3 sets of 6-8 repetitions, focusing on lifting heavy while maintaining good form.

- Bent-Over Rows: Essential for building a strong back. Perform 3 sets of 6-8 reps, ensuring you pull with your back muscles rather than just your arms.

- Shoulder Press: Either with dumbbells or a barbell, this exercise targets the shoulders and triceps. Do 3 sets of 6-8 reps.

- Pull-Ups or Lat Pull-Downs: Great for the lats and overall upper body strength. Aim for 3 sets to failure if doing pull-ups or 3 sets of 8-10 reps for lat pull-downs.

- Bicep Curls: A focused movement for bicep development. Perform 3 sets of 8-12 reps.

- Tricep Dips or Tricep Pushdowns: Finish the workout with tricep-focused exercises, aiming for 3 sets of 8-12 reps.

For the lower body workout, the emphasis is on the quadriceps, hamstrings, glutes, and calves. These workouts typically involve heavy and intense leg exercises, capitalizing on the lower body's capacity for strength. An example of a lower body workout could include:

- Squats: The king of lower body exercises. Perform 3 sets of 6-8 reps, focusing on depth and form.

- Deadlifts: A full-body exercise that heavily involves the lower back, glutes, and hamstrings. Do 3 sets of 6-8 reps.

- Leg Press: Useful for targeting the quadriceps and glutes, especially when squats are too taxing. Aim for 3 sets of 10-12 reps.

- Lunges: Walking lunges or stationary lunges work the entire leg. Do 3 sets of 10 reps per leg.

- Leg Curls: Focus on the hamstrings with 3 sets of 10-12 reps.

- Calf Raises: Finish the session by targeting the calves with 3 sets of 15-20 reps.

These workouts in the upper/lower split allow for a balanced approach to strength training, ensuring that all major muscle groups are worked evenly and effectively. The split also provides enough flexibility for individuals to adjust exercises, sets, and reps according to their fitness levels and goals. For those looking to increase intensity, advanced techniques like supersets, drop sets, or increasing the weight can be incorporated.

Incorporating the upper/lower split into a weekly routine offers an effective way to build strength and muscle in a structured manner. By focusing on upper body exercises in one session and lower body exercises in another, it ensures comprehensive muscle development and adequate recovery time. This split is adaptable, allowing individuals to tailor their workouts to their specific needs, whether they're aiming to increase muscle mass, improve strength, or enhance overall fitness.

Push/Pull/Legs Split

The push/pull/legs split is a highly regarded and efficient workout structure that has gained substantial popularity in the fitness community. This method categorizes exercises based on primary movement patterns, creating a well-rounded and balanced training regimen. This split is particularly favored for its ability to optimize training while ensuring comprehensive muscle engagement.

The framework of the push/pull/legs split is straightforward yet effective. It divides workouts into three distinct categories: push workouts, pull workouts, and legs workouts. Push workouts focus on exercises that involve pushing movements, primarily targeting the chest, shoulders, and triceps. Typical exercises include bench presses, overhead presses, and push-ups. These workouts are designed to maximize the development of the anterior (front) upper body muscles.

Pull workouts, on the other hand, revolve around pulling movements. These sessions primarily engage the back, biceps, and forearms. Exercises commonly found in pull workouts include pull-ups, rows, and deadlifts. The emphasis is on the posterior (back) upper body muscles, ensuring a balanced development in conjunction with the push workouts.

Legs workouts are dedicated exclusively to the lower body. This category includes exercises that target the quadriceps, hamstrings, glutes, and calves. Key exercises in leg workouts include squats, lunges, and calf raises. These sessions are crucial for building lower body strength and symmetry with the upper body muscle groups.

Typically, the push/pull/legs split is executed over a three-day or six-day cycle. The three-day cycle is suitable for those with limited time or those who prefer longer recovery periods. It involves one day each for push, pull, and legs workouts, with rest or active recovery days in between. The six-day cycle doubles the frequency, allowing each muscle group to be worked twice a week. This higher frequency can lead to faster strength gains and muscle growth, but it requires a higher level of fitness and recovery capability.

One of the primary benefits of the push/pull/legs split is balanced muscle development. By categorizing workouts based on movement patterns, it ensures that all major muscle groups are worked evenly. This balanced approach prevents muscle imbalances and fosters a harmonious physique. It's particularly beneficial for those aiming for aesthetic improvements as well as functional strength.

Versatility is another significant advantage of this split. It can be adapted to various frequencies to accommodate different schedules and recovery needs. Whether an individual can commit to three days or six days of training per week, the push/pull/legs split can be modified accordingly. This flexibility makes it a viable option for a wide range of individuals, from busy professionals to dedicated athletes.

Focused intensity is a key characteristic of each workout day in the push/pull/legs split. By concentrating on specific muscle groups each session, it allows for a more intense and effective workout. This focus enhances muscle fatigue and growth within each group, leading to more efficient training sessions. It also allows for a higher volume of work for each muscle group, a critical factor for hypertrophy and strength gains.

Lastly, the split minimizes the chances of muscle overuse and fatigue. Since each muscle group is worked independently on different days, there's a reduced risk of overtraining. This separation allows for adequate recovery for each muscle group, which is crucial for muscle repair, growth, and overall workout effectiveness.

The push/pull/legs split is a structured approach to strength training, dividing workouts into three distinct categories – push, pull, and legs – each targeting specific muscle groups. This division allows for an intense focus on each muscle group, leading to more effective training sessions and balanced muscle development.

Push Workout

The push workout targets muscles involved in pushing movements, primarily the chest, shoulders, and triceps. This workout typically includes:

- Bench Press: A cornerstone exercise for chest development. It also engages the triceps and shoulders. Start with 3-4 sets of 6-10 repetitions, using a weight that challenges the muscles while maintaining proper form.

- Overhead Press: This exercise targets the shoulders (deltoids) and also works the triceps. Perform 3-4 sets of 6-10 reps, choosing a weight that allows for full range of motion.

- Tricep Dips: These focus on the triceps, and can be performed using parallel bars or a bench. Aim for 3 sets of 8-12 reps.

- Incline Bench Press: This variation targets the upper chest and shoulders more than the flat bench press. Perform 3 sets of 6-10 reps.

- Side Lateral Raises: Excellent for isolating the side deltoids. Do 3 sets of 10-15 reps using lighter weights for proper form.

The push workout effectively exhausts the upper body pushing muscles, leading to improved strength and size in these areas.

Pull Workout

The pull workout focuses on the upper body pulling muscles: the back, biceps, and forearms. Key exercises include:

- Deadlifts: A compound movement that targets the entire back, including the latissimus dorsi, rhomboids, and traps. Perform 3-4 sets of 6-8 reps with a challenging weight.

- Pull-Ups: Excellent for back and bicep development. Aim for 3 sets of as many reps as possible. If too difficult, assisted pull-ups or lat pull-downs can be substituted.

- Barbell Rows: Focus on the middle and lower back. Perform 3-4 sets of 6-10 reps, ensuring you're pulling with your back muscles.

- Bicep Curls: Can be done with dumbbells or a barbell. Aim for 3 sets of 8-12 reps.

- Face Pulls: Target the rear deltoids and upper back. Perform 3 sets of 12-15 reps.

The pull workout thoroughly works the back and bicep muscles, promoting balanced development with the pushing muscles.

Legs Workout

The legs workout is dedicated to the lower body, targeting the quadriceps, hamstrings, glutes, and calves. A typical legs workout includes:

- Squats: The most comprehensive lower body exercise. Perform 3-4 sets of 6-10 reps, focusing on depth and maintaining form.

- Lunges: Work the quads, hamstrings, and glutes. Do 3 sets of 10 reps per leg.

- Leg Press: An alternative or addition to squats, targeting the quads and glutes. Aim for 3 sets of 10-12 reps.

- Romanian Deadlifts: Focus on the hamstrings and glutes. Perform 3 sets of 8-10 reps.

- Calf Raises: Essential for developing the calf muscles. Do 3 sets of 12-15 reps.

The legs workout ensures that the lower body is not neglected, providing a balanced approach to full-body development.

Each of these workouts in the push/pull/legs split allows for targeted muscle development and strength gains. By focusing on specific muscle groups in each session, the split ensures comprehensive development across all major muscle groups. The routine can be adapted in terms of the number of sets, repetitions, and weights used to suit individual fitness levels and goals.

Ideal Candidates for the Push/Pull/Legs Split

The push/pull/legs split is a highly versatile workout regimen well-suited for certain types of trainees due to its specific structure and intense focus on different muscle groups. This split is ideal for intermediate and advanced trainees, individuals with flexible schedules, and those with goal-specific training targets such as building strength, hypertrophy, or muscle definition.

Intermediate and Advanced Trainees

Intermediate and advanced trainees often reach a point in their fitness journey where generalized workouts no longer yield the same level of results as before. These individuals require a more specific and intense focus on each muscle group to continue progressing. The push/pull/legs split meets this need perfectly, as it allows for an intense workout of each muscle group before moving on to the next. This split provides the opportunity to focus on heavier lifts and more complex movements that are crucial for continued muscle development and strength gains. Since each workout day is dedicated to a specific set of muscles, it's easier to target weaknesses and work on specific areas for balanced, overall development.

Individuals with a Flexible Schedule

The push/pull/legs split is highly adaptable, making it suitable for individuals with varying schedules. For those who can commit to a six-day workout cycle, this split allows each muscle group to be worked twice a week, accelerating progress in strength and hypertrophy. Alternatively, for those with tighter schedules or who require more recovery time, the split can be adjusted to a three-day cycle. This flexibility is a significant advantage, as it allows individuals to tailor their workout routine to their lifestyle without compromising the effectiveness of their training program. The ability to adjust the frequency also means that the split can accommodate changes in an individual's life, be it due to work, family commitments, or other responsibilities.

Goal-Specific Trainees

Individuals with specific fitness goals such as building strength, increasing muscle size (hypertrophy), or enhancing overall muscle definition find the push/pull/legs split particularly beneficial. This workout structure allows for focused and intense training sessions that are key to these goals. For strength and hypertrophy, the split supports high-volume and high-intensity workouts, crucial for stimulating muscle growth and strength improvement. The separation of muscle groups ensures that each group is thoroughly exhausted in its workout, an essential factor in muscle hypertrophy.

Furthermore, for those focusing on muscle definition, this split allows for targeted exercises that can sculpt and define various muscle groups. The ability to concentrate on specific areas in each workout ensures that all muscles are developed evenly, contributing to a more defined and aesthetic physique.

The Bro Split

The "bro split" stands as a classic, time-tested approach to strength training and bodybuilding. Its roots run deep in the fitness community, where it has been embraced for its intense focus on individual muscle groups. The bro split dedicates each day of the week to training a specific muscle group, typically spread over five to six days. This structure allows for highly focused and intense workouts for each muscle group, providing ample time for recovery before the same group is worked again.

The bro split's primary appeal lies in its intense muscle focus. This split allows for a high volume and intensity of training for each muscle group. For example, a typical bro split routine might dedicate one day entirely to chest exercises, another to back, and so on. This approach ensures that each muscle group is thoroughly worked during its dedicated session, leading to significant muscle fatigue and subsequent growth. This focus is particularly beneficial for those looking to increase muscle size and definition, as it allows for targeted development of each muscle group.

Simplicity is another key advantage of the bro split. Its straightforward structure is easy to understand and follow, making it an attractive option for both beginners and experienced gym-goers. This simplicity also aids in maintaining a routine, as there's no confusion about what muscle group to work on any given day. For beginners, it provides a clear roadmap for navigating the gym, and for the experienced, it allows for a well-structured approach to their training.

Customization is a significant aspect of the bro split. It allows for a high degree of personalization in choosing exercises for each muscle group. Depending on individual preferences, goals, and needs, exercises can be selected to target different aspects of each muscle group. For instance, on chest day, one could focus on flat bench presses, incline presses, and flyes, tailoring the workout to specific chest areas.

One of the most critical aspects of the bro split is the recovery time it affords each muscle group. By working each muscle group intensely once a week, the split provides a full week of recovery before that group is worked again. This extended recovery period is beneficial for muscle growth and repair, as muscles need time to recover and grow after being subjected to intense training. It's during this recovery period that the actual process of muscle building occurs.

The bro split's focus on one muscle group per day also allows for a more extended workout for each group. This can lead to increased muscle exhaustion and, consequently, growth. For example, dedicating an entire session to the back allows for a variety of exercises targeting different back parts, such as the latissimus dorsi, rhomboids, and trapezius muscles. This variety ensures comprehensive development of the muscle group and can lead to more pronounced muscle gains.

Additionally, the bro split's structure aids in preventing burnout and overtraining. By concentrating on one muscle group per session, the risk of overworking a muscle group is significantly reduced. This approach allows for more focused energy and effort during each workout, as only one major muscle group is being taxed per session.

However, the bro split requires a significant time commitment, as it typically involves training five to six days a week. This commitment can be challenging for those with busy schedules or limited time for gym sessions. Despite this, for those who can dedicate the necessary time, the bro split offers a highly effective way to build muscle and strength.

Example Workout Routine

The bro split routine is a classic approach in bodybuilding and strength training circles, targeting one major muscle group each day of the week. This approach allows for an intense focus on each muscle group, providing ample time for recovery before the same group is worked again. A sample weekly bro split routine can be structured as follows:

Monday: Chest Day

- Bench Press: Begin with 3-4 sets of 6-8 reps. The bench press is a staple in chest development, targeting the pectorals, triceps, and front deltoids.

- Incline Dumbbell Press: Perform 3 sets of 8-10 reps. This exercise focuses on the upper chest, promoting a balanced chest development.

- Chest Flyes: Do 3 sets of 10-12 reps. Flyes help to stretch and isolate the chest muscles, enhancing muscle definition.

Tuesday: Back Day

- Pull-Ups: Aim for 3-4 sets to failure. Pull-ups are excellent for overall back development, particularly targeting the latissimus dorsi.

- Bent-Over Rows: Complete 3 sets of 6-8 reps. This exercise strengthens the middle back muscles and contributes to overall back thickness.

- Lat Pulldowns: Do 3 sets of 8-10 reps. Lat pulldowns focus on the width of the back, particularly the lats.

Wednesday: Shoulders Day

- Overhead Press: Start with 3-4 sets of 6-8 reps. The overhead press is crucial for building overall shoulder strength and size.

- Lateral Raises: Perform 3 sets of 10-12 reps. Lateral raises target the side deltoids, essential for shoulder width and definition.

- Front Raises: Do 3 sets of 10-12 reps. This exercise targets the front deltoids, rounding out shoulder development.

Thursday: Arms Day

- Bicep Curls: Perform 3 sets of 8-10 reps. Bicep curls are fundamental for building arm size and strength.

- Tricep Extensions: Complete 3 sets of 8-10 reps. Tricep extensions target the triceps muscles, crucial for overall arm development.

- Hammer Curls: Do 3 sets of 10-12 reps. Hammer curls focus on the brachialis and brachioradialis, enhancing arm thickness and strength.

Friday: Legs Day

- Squats: Begin with 3-4 sets of 6-8 reps. Squats are essential for overall leg development, particularly the quadriceps and glutes.

- Deadlifts: Perform 3 sets of 6-8 reps. Deadlifts target the entire posterior chain, including the hamstrings, glutes, and lower back.

- Leg Presses: Complete 3 sets of 10-12 reps. The leg press is a great complement to squats, targeting the quads and glutes with less strain on the lower back.

Saturday: Rest or Optional Focus on a Weak Muscle Group

This day can be used for rest or to focus on a weaker muscle group that needs additional attention. If choosing to train, select 2-3 exercises for the targeted muscle group and perform a moderate workout, being mindful not to overtrain.

Sunday: Rest

Dedicate this day to complete rest, allowing your body to recover, repair, and grow stronger. Rest is a critical component of any training routine, particularly one as intense as the bro split.

This sample weekly bro split routine offers a comprehensive approach to muscle building, with each day dedicated to enhancing a specific muscle group. It's crucial to ensure proper form and adequate recovery between sets and exercises. Additionally, listen to your body and make adjustments as needed based on your recovery and overall fitness progress.

Ideal Candidates for the Bro Split

The bro split, known for its intense focus on individual muscle groups, is a workout regimen that resonates with specific segments of the fitness community. Its structure, which dedicates each day to a different muscle group, makes it particularly suitable for certain types of individuals, such as bodybuilders, experienced lifters, those with flexible schedules, and recovery-oriented trainees.

Bodybuilders and Muscle Builders

The bro split is ideal for bodybuilders and those focusing on muscle hypertrophy and definition. This split's structure allows for an intensive workout on each muscle group, leading to significant muscle fatigue and growth. By dedicating an entire day to one muscle group, individuals can perform a high volume of exercises targeting various aspects of that muscle, which is crucial for hypertrophy. The bro split also allows for a focus on muscle definition. The ability to concentrate on one muscle group at a time enables lifters to perform isolation exercises that enhance muscle shape and definition, a key goal in bodybuilding.

Experienced Lifters

Experienced lifters, who already have a solid foundation in strength training, find the bro split particularly effective. These individuals are typically capable of handling high-volume and high-intensity workouts that the bro split demands. Having developed a base level of strength and muscle endurance, they can benefit from the intensive nature of the bro split, which can lead to further strength gains and muscle development. Experienced lifters often have the technique and stamina necessary to withstand the rigors of this type of training, making the bro split a suitable choice for their advanced training needs.

Those with Flexible Schedules

The bro split is best suited for individuals who can dedicate five to six days a week to their workout routine. Due to its structure, the bro split requires a significant time commitment, with each workout day focusing on a different muscle group. This frequency is essential for the split's effectiveness, as it ensures that each muscle group is thoroughly worked each week. Individuals with the flexibility to commit to this type of schedule will find the bro split to be a practical and efficient way to structure their workouts.

Recovery-Oriented Trainees

Trainees who require or prefer longer recovery periods for each muscle group will find the bro split beneficial. Since each muscle group is worked intensely only once a week, there is ample time for recovery before that group is targeted again. This extended recovery time can be advantageous for muscle repair and growth. For individuals who need more time to recover due to their physiological makeup, age, or other factors, the bro split provides the necessary rest period for each muscle

The 5x5 Split

The 5x5 training program is a paradigm of strength training, valued for its straightforward yet highly effective approach. Centering on five sets of five repetitions of key compound lifts, this program is not just about building muscle; it's a comprehensive method to enhance overall strength and athletic performance. The 5x5 program is a testament to the principle that in simplicity lies power. This regimen revolves around a select few compound exercises, each performed with heavy weights. The core idea is to engage multiple muscle groups simultaneously, making every session both time-efficient and potent.

Compound exercises are the linchpin of the 5x5 program. These movements, such as squats, deadlifts, bench presses, and overhead presses, work several muscle groups at once. Unlike isolation exercises that target individual muscles, compound movements recruit large muscle areas, offering a more holistic approach to strength building. This method not only accelerates muscle growth but also enhances functional strength – the kind of strength that is useful in everyday life.

Squats, for instance, engage the quadriceps, hamstrings, glutes, lower back, and core, making them an incredibly effective lower body exercise. The deadlift, another staple of the 5x5 program, works almost every major muscle group, including the back, glutes, legs, and core. The bench press and overhead press are critical for developing the upper body, targeting the chest, shoulders, and triceps. These exercises combined provide a balanced workout that strengthens the entire body.

A key feature of the 5x5 program is its emphasis on progressive overload, a crucial principle in strength training. Progressive overload involves gradually increasing the weight lifted to challenge the muscles continuously. This approach is critical for muscle growth and strength improvement. In the context of the 5x5 program, once an individual can complete five sets of five reps with a certain weight, they increase the weight slightly in the next workout. This gradual increase ensures steady progress and minimizes the risk of injury.

The 5x5 program is also marked by its simplicity, both in terms of the exercises involved and its implementation. With only a handful of exercises to focus on, it's easier for individuals to track their progress and maintain consistency. This simplicity is especially beneficial for beginners who can often be overwhelmed by more complex routines. For the experienced lifter, the straightforward nature of the program provides a clear structure for continued development.

However, the simplicity of the 5x5 program doesn't imply that it's easy. The workouts can be quite challenging, particularly as the weights increase. The five sets of five reps scheme requires a significant amount of physical and mental endurance. This aspect of the program builds not just muscle, but also grit and determination, qualities that are invaluable in any fitness journey.

The 5x5 program is also adaptable. While the traditional 5x5 split focuses on three workouts per week, it can be adjusted according to individual needs and schedules. For example, someone with more time and recovery capability might add a fourth day focusing on accessory exercises or additional cardiovascular work. Conversely, for someone pressed for time, the program can be condensed into two longer workouts per week.

This training regimen is particularly well-suited for those looking to gain strength in a structured and measurable way. It is ideal for beginners to intermediate lifters, though advanced lifters can also benefit significantly by returning to this fundamental strength-building approach. The 5x5 program is not just about lifting weights; it's about building a solid foundation upon which other fitness goals can be achieved.

In essence, the 5x5 program is a powerful tool in the arsenal of strength training. Its focus on compound movements, progressive overload, and simplicity makes it an effective and efficient method for building strength and muscle. This program proves that sometimes, the most straightforward approaches can be the most impactful, providing a clear path to greater strength and overall fitness.

Example 5x5 Workouts

The 5x5 workout program, renowned for its simplicity and effectiveness, revolves around two primary workout routines – Workout A and Workout B. These routines are alternated three times a week, focusing on major compound movements that engage multiple muscle groups. The essence of the 5x5 program lies in its structured approach, performing five sets of five reps for each exercise, except for deadlifts, which due to their intensity, are typically performed for one set of five reps.

Workout A

- Squat: The squat is a fundamental exercise in the 5x5 program. It targets the quadriceps, hamstrings, glutes, lower back, and core. For the 5x5 routine, you perform five sets of five reps. The focus should be on maintaining proper form, keeping the back straight, and driving through the heels. As a full-body compound movement, it not only builds lower body strength but also contributes to overall muscle growth and development.

- Bench Press: Next in Workout A is the bench press, which primarily works the chest muscles (pectorals), as well as the triceps and shoulders (deltoids). Again, five sets of five reps are performed. Proper form includes lying flat on the bench, feet firmly on the ground, and controlling the barbell as it's lowered to the chest and pushed back up. The bench press is key for upper body strength and is a staple in strength training.

- Barbell Row: The barbell row focuses on the upper back, including the latissimus dorsi, rhomboids, and trapezius muscles, as well as the biceps. It's crucial for maintaining balance in the body's musculature, countering the pushing movements of the bench press. Perform five sets of five reps, maintaining a bent-over position with a straight back, pulling the barbell towards the lower ribs, and then lowering it under control.

Workout B

- Squat: As in Workout A, the squat is also the first exercise in Workout B, highlighting its importance in the program. The same approach is followed – five sets of five reps, focusing on depth, form, and control. Consistent performance of squats is crucial for lower body strength and overall athletic ability.

- Overhead Press: The overhead press, or military press, targets the shoulders, triceps, and upper back. This exercise is performed standing, pressing the barbell from shoulder height above the head. Five sets of five reps are done, ensuring that each rep involves a full range of motion from shoulders to lockout above the head. The overhead press is essential for building strong, functional shoulders and arms.

- Deadlift: The deadlift is a powerful compound exercise that targets the entire posterior chain, including the hamstrings, glutes, lower and upper back. Due to its intensity, only one set of five reps is performed in the 5x5 program. Proper form is crucial to avoid injury – keeping the back straight, lifting with the legs and hips, and keeping the barbell close to the body throughout the lift.

In both Workout A and Workout B, the weights used should be challenging yet manageable to complete all sets and reps with proper form. The 5x5 program is designed for progressive overload, meaning that as you grow stronger, you should gradually increase the weight used in each exercise. This progression is key to the effectiveness of the 5x5 program, driving consistent strength and muscle gains.

These workouts encapsulate the essence of strength training – focusing on major compound movements, challenging the body, and promoting growth. The simplicity of the 5x5 program makes it highly effective, ensuring a balanced approach to building foundational strength.

Benefits of Strength-Focused Splits

Strength-focused workout splits, particularly the renowned 5x5 program, offer a plethora of benefits for a wide demographic, ranging from beginners to seasoned athletes. These splits, known for their simplicity and effectiveness, are designed to build foundational strength that is applicable to both sports and daily activities. They provide a structured pathway for increasing muscle strength, enhancing bone and joint health, boosting metabolism, and improving athletic performance.

One of the most significant benefits of strength-focused splits like the 5x5 program is the increased muscle strength. This type of training regimen emphasizes heavy lifting with compound movements, which are key to developing overall muscular strength. Compound exercises such as squats, deadlifts, and bench presses target multiple muscle groups simultaneously, allowing for a more efficient strength-building workout. Increased muscle strength is not only beneficial for enhancing physical appearance but is also crucial in improving daily functional abilities, such as lifting heavy objects, pushing or pulling items, and maintaining overall body stability.

Another crucial benefit of these workout splits is their positive impact on bone and joint health. Strength training is known to enhance bone density, which is especially important as one ages. Regularly performing weight-bearing exercises helps in combating age-related bone loss, reducing the risk of osteoporosis, and other bone-related conditions. Furthermore, by strengthening the muscles around the joints, these workouts contribute to joint stability, which can help prevent injuries and improve overall joint health.

Metabolic boost is another key advantage of engaging in strength-focused workout splits. Strength training has been shown to elevate metabolism, aiding in fat loss and muscle maintenance. This metabolic increase occurs because muscle tissue burns more calories at rest compared to fat tissue. Therefore, by increasing muscle mass through strength training, one can elevate their resting metabolic rate, making it easier to maintain a healthy body weight or lose fat if that's a personal goal.

Improved athletic performance is a direct outcome of engaging in a strength-focused training regimen. Strength gains achieved through these workouts translate to better performance in almost every athletic endeavor, be it running, swimming, cycling, or team sports. Enhanced muscle strength and endurance allow athletes to perform at a higher level, improve their technique, and reduce the risk of sport-related injuries.

The 5x5 workout split, in particular, is excellent for strength training beginners due to its straightforward approach. This program simplifies strength training into a manageable format, focusing on a few key exercises and requiring only three workouts per week. For someone new to strength training, this simplicity eliminates the often overwhelming complexity of more intricate workout routines, providing a clear and concise pathway to gaining strength and confidence in the gym.

Athletes, regardless of their sport, can benefit immensely from the 5x5 split. For competitive sports, a strong foundation of muscular strength is often a prerequisite for peak performance. The 5x5 program offers a focused approach to building this foundation, ensuring athletes develop the strength needed to excel in their respective sports.

Individuals with limited time find the 5x5 split ideal. Since the program is designed for efficiency, requiring only three days a week, it's suitable for those with busy schedules. Each workout in the 5x5 program is concise yet effective, focusing on a few compound exercises that provide a full-body workout in a relatively short period.

Lastly, the 5x5 split is suitable for anyone seeking to improve their overall functional fitness and core strength. This program not only builds muscle in the traditional sense but also enhances the body's ability to perform everyday activities more efficiently and with less risk of injury. The focus on compound movements ensures that the core and stabilizing muscles are engaged, which is crucial for overall functional strength.

In summary, strength-focused splits, and particularly the 5x5 program, are beneficial for a wide range of individuals. They offer a structured approach to increasing muscle strength, enhancing bone and joint health, boosting metabolism, and improving athletic performance. These splits are ideal for beginners, athletes, individuals with limited time, and those seeking functional strength, making them a versatile tool in achieving various fitness goals.

Hybrid and Custom Splits

Hybrid and custom workout splits represent an innovative approach to fitness training, offering unparalleled flexibility and personalization. These types of splits are tailored to individual needs, blending elements from traditional workout splits to create a unique fitness regimen. This approach is particularly beneficial for individuals with specific goals, varied interests, or unique scheduling needs.

The concept of hybrid and custom splits is rooted in the idea that no one-size-fits-all solution exists for fitness training. Every individual has unique goals, preferences, body types, and lifestyles, all of which should be considered when designing a workout plan. Hybrid splits allow for the combination of different training styles and methodologies. For example, someone might combine elements of a body part split (like the bro split) with full-body workout days. This could mean dedicating specific days to focus intensely on one muscle group while incorporating full-body workouts on other days for balanced development.

Designing a custom split requires a thoughtful assessment of personal goals. For instance, someone aiming to build strength might focus more on heavy compound exercises, whereas someone interested in muscle toning might incorporate a mix of weightlifting and high-repetition training. Endurance enhancement might call for integrating cardiovascular exercises, while weight loss could involve a combination of strength training and high-intensity interval training (HIIT). Understanding these goals is crucial in shaping the structure of the workout split.

An individual's lifestyle and time availability play a significant role in designing a custom split. For those with demanding jobs or family commitments, a workout split needs to be efficient and flexible. For example, a busy professional might opt for shorter, more intense workout sessions or fewer training days with longer workouts. Similarly, someone with a more flexible schedule might choose a split that allows for more frequent but shorter sessions.

Recovery capability is another critical factor. The workout split should provide enough time for rest and muscle recovery, which is essential for growth and preventing overtraining. This consideration might lead to alternating between intense workout days and lighter or active recovery days.

The incorporation of varied training styles is a hallmark of hybrid and custom splits. This variety not only keeps the workouts interesting and challenging but also ensures that all major muscle groups are worked. For instance, someone might combine powerlifting exercises for strength with bodybuilding techniques for hypertrophy and some elements of functional training for overall fitness.

Ensuring comprehensive development of all muscle groups is essential in a hybrid or custom split. This means that while the split might focus on certain areas or goals, it should still provide a balanced workout regimen. For example, if someone's primary focus is on upper body strength, they should still incorporate lower body and core exercises to prevent imbalances and maintain overall fitness.

Hybrid and custom splits also allow for specific tailoring to address individual weaknesses or preferences. For example, if someone has a weaker lower back, they can incorporate specific exercises to strengthen that area. Similarly, if someone prefers certain types of exercises or equipment, those can be integrated into their custom plan.

Flexibility in adjusting the split over time is another advantage. As individuals progress in their fitness journey, their goals and needs might change. A custom or hybrid split can be easily modified to accommodate these changes, whether it's increasing the intensity, changing the focus, or incorporating new exercises.

In summary, hybrid and custom workout splits offer a personalized approach to fitness training. By blending elements from different splits and tailoring them to individual needs and goals, these splits provide a flexible and effective way to achieve fitness objectives. Whether it's building strength, enhancing muscle tone, improving endurance, or losing weight, hybrid and custom splits offer a tailored pathway to reach these goals while ensuring a balanced and comprehensive approach to physical development.

Examples of Hybrid Splits

Hybrid workout splits represent a modern and adaptable approach to fitness, combining elements from various established training methods to suit individual needs and goals. These hybrid splits provide the flexibility to focus on specific areas while maintaining a holistic approach to fitness. Let's delve into some examples of hybrid splits and how they can be structured.

Upper/Lower + Full Body Split

This hybrid split merges the focus of an upper/lower split with the comprehensive approach of full-body workouts. In a typical week, a trainee might alternate between upper/lower body days and full-body workout days. This structure allows for concentrated effort on specific muscle groups during the upper/lower days, while full-body days ensure all muscle groups are engaged within the same session.

For example, the week might begin with an upper body workout on Monday, focusing on exercises like bench presses and pull-ups. Tuesday could then shift to a lower body workout with squats and deadlifts. Wednesday might be a rest or active recovery day, followed by a full-body workout on Thursday, incorporating a mix of upper and lower body exercises. The cycle could then repeat or mix in additional rest days, depending on the individual's recovery needs and schedule.

Push/Pull/Legs + Bro Split Hybrid

This hybrid split combines the push/pull/legs framework with elements of the bro split, dedicating specific days to individual muscle groups. This structure allows for a balance between focused muscle group training and comprehensive workouts. For example, a week might start with a push workout (chest, shoulders, triceps) on Monday, followed by a pull workout (back, biceps) on Tuesday, and a legs workout (quadriceps, hamstrings, calves) on Wednesday.

The latter part of the week could then shift to a bro split approach, with Thursday dedicated to chest, Friday to back, and Saturday to arms. This hybrid split allows for intense focus on each muscle group while still maintaining the balanced approach of the push/pull/legs split.

5x5 + Functional Training Split

This hybrid combines the strength-focused 5x5 program, known for its simplicity and effectiveness in building strength, with functional training exercises to enhance athletic performance. The 5x5 portion of the workout, which includes exercises like squats, deadlifts, and bench presses, could be performed three days a week – for example, Monday, Wednesday, and Friday.

On alternate days, functional training exercises could be incorporated. These exercises focus on movements that mimic daily activities or sports-specific movements, improving overall athletic ability and functional strength. Such workouts might include kettlebell swings, medicine ball throws, or plyometric exercises. This combination ensures the development of raw strength while also enhancing agility, balance, and coordination.

Endurance and Strength Split

This hybrid split is ideal for those looking to balance endurance training with strength training. It's particularly suitable for athletes in sports that require both strength and endurance, such as obstacle course racing or triathlon. In this split, endurance training sessions (such as running, cycling, or swimming) could be alternated with strength training workouts.

A typical week might include endurance training on Monday, Wednesday, and Friday, focusing on different aspects such as speed, distance, and recovery pace. Strength training sessions on Tuesday, Thursday, and Saturday would then focus on full-body strength workouts, ensuring that all major muscle groups are targeted. This split allows for the development of both cardiovascular endurance and muscular strength, contributing to overall athletic performance and fitness.

In summary, hybrid workout splits offer a versatile approach to fitness training, allowing individuals to tailor their workouts to their specific goals and preferences. Whether the goal is to build muscle, enhance athletic performance, or achieve a balance of strength and endurance, hybrid splits provide a structured yet flexible framework to achieve these objectives. These examples demonstrate the adaptability of hybrid splits, accommodating a wide range of fitness levels and goals.

The Benefits of Personalized Splits

Personalized workout splits, encompassing both hybrid and custom splits, represent a cutting-edge approach in the fitness realm. These splits are designed to cater directly to individual needs, preferences, and goals, offering a multitude of benefits that standard, one-size-fits-all routines fail to provide. The primary advantages of these personalized splits include targeted results, adaptability, enhanced motivation, and the potential for holistic development.

Targeted Results

One of the most compelling reasons for adopting a personalized workout split is the ability to achieve targeted results. Each individual has unique fitness goals, whether it's building muscle, increasing endurance, losing weight, or improving athletic performance. A personalized split allows for the creation of a workout routine that directly aligns with these specific objectives. For instance, someone aiming for muscle hypertrophy might focus more on weightlifting and high-volume workouts, while an endurance athlete would integrate more cardiovascular exercises into their split. This tailored approach ensures that every minute spent in the gym is optimized towards achieving the desired outcome.

Adaptability

Personalized workout splits offer unparalleled adaptability. Life is dynamic, and circumstances can change rapidly, impacting one's ability to stick to a rigid workout schedule. Custom splits can be easily modified to accommodate changes in lifestyle, time availability, or fitness level. For example, if an individual's work schedule becomes more demanding, the split can be adjusted to shorter, more intense workouts, or if an injury occurs, the routine can be altered to focus on recovery and exercises that do not strain the affected area. This flexibility is not just a matter of convenience; it's crucial for maintaining consistent progress in the face of life's unpredictable nature.

Enhanced Motivation

Customization in workout routines keeps the training process engaging and relevant, which is vital for sustained motivation. Doing the same exercises week after week can lead to boredom and a plateau in progress. Personalized splits allow for variety and creativity in workouts, keeping the individual engaged and challenged. This might involve mixing different types of training, such as incorporating elements of powerlifting into a bodybuilding routine or blending yoga and mobility work into a strength training program. This variety not only makes workouts more enjoyable but also ensures that different aspects of fitness are being developed.

Holistic Development

Personalized splits offer the potential for a well-rounded approach to fitness. Standard workout routines often focus on specific goals, like muscle building or cardiovascular endurance, which can lead to imbalances in development. Custom splits, on the other hand, can be designed to address all aspects of fitness – strength, endurance, flexibility, and balance – leading to a more holistic development. This approach is crucial for overall health and wellness and can significantly reduce the risk of injuries that often result from imbalances or overemphasis on certain types of training.

Ideal Candidates for Hybrid and Custom Splits

- Experienced Gym-Goers: Individuals who have spent considerable time in the gym and understand their bodies and fitness needs are ideal candidates for hybrid and custom splits. These individuals have the knowledge to mix different training styles effectively, tailoring their routines to their evolving goals and preferences.

- Goal-Specific Athletes: Athletes training for specific sports or events require workout routines that address the particular demands of their sport. Personalized splits allow these athletes to focus on the aspects of fitness that will most enhance their performance in their chosen sport, be it strength, speed, agility, or endurance.

- People with Unique Schedules: Those whose lifestyles demand flexibility in their workout routines can greatly benefit from custom splits. Be it working parents, traveling professionals, or students balancing studies and fitness, personalized splits offer the adaptability needed to fit workouts into diverse and often changing schedules.

- Fitness Enthusiasts Seeking Variety: For those who enjoy exploring different aspects of fitness and dislike the monotony of standard routines, personalized splits offer an opportunity to diversify their training. This might involve experimenting with new exercises, incorporating different training methodologies, or adjusting the routine to align with changing fitness interests.

Personalized workout splits offer a range of benefits that standard workout programs often fail to provide. Their ability to deliver targeted results, adaptability to changing circumstances, enhancement of motivation through customization, and the potential for holistic development make them an excellent choice for a wide array of individuals. From experienced gym-goers and specific-goal athletes to people with unique schedules and fitness enthusiasts seeking variety, personalized workout splits present a flexible and effective solution for achieving diverse fitness goals.

Navigating the Complexities of Workout Splits

In the realm of fitness and bodybuilding, workout splits are a fundamental concept, often surrounded by questions and misconceptions. This chapter aims to provide clarity and guidance on navigating the complexities of workout splits, offering answers to frequently asked questions, debunking common misconceptions, and providing tips to avoid typical mistakes.

Frequently Asked Questions

- Changing Workout Splits: How often one should change their workout split depends on several factors, including progress, boredom, and adaptation. Generally, it's advisable to change your split every 8-12 weeks to prevent plateaus and keep the training stimulus fresh. However, if a split is still yielding results and remains enjoyable, it's perfectly fine to stick with it longer.

- Cardio on Rest Days: Incorporating light to moderate cardio on rest days can be beneficial. It keeps the body active and can aid in recovery by increasing blood flow to the muscles. However, it's important to ensure that this doesn't compromise recovery by being too intense or lengthy.

- Necessity of Specific Splits for Results: While workout splits can be highly effective, they are not the only way to achieve fitness results. The key to success in any training program is consistency, proper nutrition, and a workout plan that aligns with one's goals, whether it's a split routine or a full-body approach.

- Determining the Right Split: Choosing the right workout split involves considering factors such as fitness goals, experience level, schedule, and personal preferences. It's essential to select a split that not only aligns with your goals but is also realistic in terms of your time commitment and enjoyment.

- Combining Different Workout Splits: Yes, it's possible to combine different types of workout splits. This approach, often seen in hybrid splits, allows for more customization and can address specific training goals or preferences. For example, one could combine elements of a push/pull/legs split with full-body workouts.

Debunking Common Misconceptions

- More Gym Time Equals Better Results: Quality over quantity is crucial in fitness. Longer or more frequent gym sessions don't necessarily lead to better results and can sometimes lead to overtraining or burnout.

- Sticking to One Workout Split: While consistency is important, it's not mandatory to stick to one workout split indefinitely. Changing your split can provide new challenges and stimuli to the muscles, aiding in continued progress.

- Heavier Weights Are Always Better: While lifting heavy is important for strength and muscle building, it's not the only way to achieve results. Different rep ranges and intensities have their place in a well-rounded fitness program.

- Rest Days for Complete Inactivity: Rest days are essential for recovery, but they don't necessarily mean complete inactivity. Active recovery, such as light cardio, stretching, or yoga, can be beneficial.

Tips to Avoid Common Mistakes in Workout Splits

- Not Allowing Adequate Recovery: Underestimating the importance of rest can lead to overtraining and hinder progress. It's essential to include rest days in your split and listen to your body for signs of fatigue.

- Ignoring Nutrition and Hydration: Both play a crucial role in supporting your workout split. Proper nutrition fuels your workouts and aids in recovery, while staying hydrated is key for overall health and exercise performance.

- Lack of Consistency: Sticking to a workout routine is fundamental for seeing results. Consistency trumps perfection, and being regular with your workouts is more important than waiting for the 'perfect' time or conditions.

- Imbalanced Training: Focusing too much on certain muscle groups and neglecting others can lead to imbalances and injuries. Ensure your split addresses all major muscle groups evenly.

- Ignoring Form and Technique: Proper form and technique are essential for preventing injuries and getting the most out of your exercises. Always prioritize form over the amount of weight lifted.

Fine-Tuning Your Workout Split

- Listening to Your Body: Be attentive to what your body tells you. If you feel overly fatigued or experience pain (beyond normal muscle soreness), it may be time to adjust your split or intensity.

- Seeking Professional Guidance: Especially when starting a new split or if you hit a plateau, consulting with a fitness professional can provide valuable insights and guidance.

Incorporating Feedback into Your Routine

- Adapting to Changes: Be prepared to modify your workout split in response to changes in your fitness levels, goals, or life circumstances. Flexibility in your approach will help maintain progress.

- Learning from Experience: Both your own experiences and those of others can be insightful. Continually refine your approach based on what you learn about your body and its response to different training stimuli.

In navigating the world of workout splits, understanding these facets is crucial. By gaining clarity on these aspects, individuals can tailor their fitness routines to be more effective, enjoyable, and aligned with

Nutrition for Optimal Performance

In the unforgiving realm of bodybuilding, where every ounce of muscle and shred of fat matters, nutrition isn't a mere afterthought—it's a weapon, a strategic advantage. Derek Lunsford, a force to be reckoned with in the world of professional bodybuilding, understands this better than most. His diet isn't a whimsical dance of exotic foods or trendy fads. No, it's a calculated and Honestly effective approach to fueling the furnace that is his body.

Derek's diet isn't about taste or indulgence; it's about purpose. It's about channeling every morsel of food into the relentless pursuit of his physique's perfection. While his diet plan might seem Spartan to some, it's the very foundation upon which his victories are built.

Let's cut straight to the chase—Derek's diet is a high-protein, low-carb affair. It's a dance of macronutrients designed to build lean muscle and torch fat. But there's more to it than just numbers on a plate. It's about precision and consistency.

Protein is the kingpin of Derek's diet. He loads up on lean protein sources like chicken, turkey, lean beef, and fish. These protein powerhouses provide the essential amino acids required for muscle growth and recovery. It's not a protein party; it's a calculated intake aimed at maintaining a positive nitrogen balance—the secret sauce for muscle building.

When it comes to carbohydrates, Derek isn't chasing after sugary treats or empty calories. He opts for complex carbs like brown rice, sweet potatoes, and quinoa. These slow-digesting carbohydrates provide a steady release of energy, allowing him to train with intensity and recover effectively.

Now, let's talk fats—essential for hormone production and overall health. Derek includes healthy fats from sources like avocados, nuts, and olive oil. These fats are the unsung heroes that keep his body functioning optimally.

But it's not just about what Derek eats; it's also about when he eats it. He's a master of meal timing, strategically consuming smaller, protein-packed meals throughout the day. This consistent fueling keeps his metabolism revving and ensures that his body never slips into a catabolic state.

Derek's diet isn't a simple matter of aesthetics. It's a critical factor in his performance and recovery. You see, bodybuilding isn't just about lifting weights; it's a grueling test of endurance, strength, and mental fortitude. And all of this hinges on nutrition.

First and foremost, Derek's diet supports muscle growth. Protein, as the cornerstone of his nutrition plan, is essential for repairing and building muscle tissue. Without adequate protein, all the lifting in the world won't yield the desired results. It's the raw material for muscle construction.

Equally important is the role of carbohydrates in his diet. These complex carbs fuel his workouts and replenish glycogen stores in his muscles. They provide the energy needed to push through Honest training sessions, lifting heavier weights and achieving progressive overload.

Fats, often maligned, play a crucial role in hormone production. Hormones like testosterone are pivotal in muscle growth, and a deficiency can hinder progress. By incorporating healthy fats, Derek ensures his hormones are firing on all cylinders.

Nutrition also plays a pivotal role in recovery. Bodybuilders like Derek push their bodies to the limit, causing muscle damage in the process. Proper nutrition is the linchpin in repairing and rebuilding these damaged muscles. Without it, the body can't bounce back as efficiently.

Now, you might be wondering how Derek manages to stick to this rigorous diet day in and day out. The answer lies in his meal planning and preparation strategies. For him, success is all about meticulous planning and unwavering discipline.

Meal planning is non-negotiable in Derek's world. He doesn't leave his nutrition to chance. Instead, he plans his meals meticulously, ensuring he hits his daily macronutrient targets. There's no room for impromptu trips to the fast-food joint; every meal is calculated.

Preparation is equally vital. Derek spends time each week prepping his meals in advance. This means cooking in bulk, portioning his meals, and storing them for easy access. When hunger strikes, there's no temptation to reach for unhealthy snacks because he has a healthy, balanced meal at the ready.

And let's not forget about hydration. Water is often overlooked, but Derek knows it's a critical component of his diet. Staying well-hydrated supports nutrient transport, digestion, and overall health. He ensures he drinks an ample amount of water throughout the day, recognizing its role in peak performance.

In the realm of bodybuilding, where success is measured in inches of muscle and ounces of body fat, Derek Lunsford's approach to nutrition is stark, methodical, and unwavering. It's not a glamorous diet, but it's a diet that gets results. In the next chapter, we'll dive into the heart of Derek's training regimen, dissecting his workouts, exercises, and training philosophy. So, brace yourself; the real work is just beginning.

In the world of bodybuilding, nutrition is your ultimate weapon, your silent partner in the quest for muscle and strength. As you sweat it out in the gym, pushing your limits with every rep, your muscles are screaming for nourishment, and it's your job to feed them. This chapter, "The Fundamentals of Bodybuilding," lays down the foundation of what it means to be a bodybuilder, and how nutrition is the very essence of your journey.

Bodybuilding isn't a mere hobby; it's a lifestyle, a relentless pursuit of physical excellence. To understand its core, we must first delve into its history. Bodybuilding, as we know it today, wasn't born yesterday. It has a rich and gritty history that traces its roots back to ancient Greece, where Herculean physiques were celebrated. But it was in the late 19th century when the sport began to take its modern form. It became a spectacle, with men and women flexing their sculpted bodies, showcasing strength, symmetry, and aesthetics. It wasn't just about being strong; it was about looking strong.

Fast forward to the present day, and bodybuilding has evolved into a multifaceted discipline. It's not just about bulging muscles and flashy poses; it's about sculpting your physique, pushing the limits of your body, and achieving the perfect blend of muscle and symmetry. It's a journey of dedication, discipline, and above all, nutrition.

You see, bodybuilding isn't a sprint; it's a marathon. And in this marathon, nutrition is your fuel. It's what powers your muscles to grow and recover. Without proper nutrition, your bodybuilding dreams are nothing but a house of cards waiting to collapse. You can lift all the weights in the world, but if you don't feed your body right, you'll never reach your true potential.

Macronutrients for Muscle Growth

In the relentless world of bodybuilding, where iron meets sweat and determination collides with the weights, nutrition isn't just a part of the puzzle – it's the bedrock on which your success is built. This chapter, "Macronutrients for Muscle Growth," is all about the raw materials that fuel your body's transformation into a powerhouse of muscle and strength. In this no-nonsense guide, we'll dive straight into the core of bodybuilding nutrition, starting with the heavyweight champion of them all: protein.

Protein: The Cornerstone of Muscle Growth

Protein isn't just another nutrient; it's your ticket to muscle city. When you're pumping iron and pushing your body to the limits, you're essentially tearing down muscle fibers. It's in the recovery phase that your muscles rebuild and grow, and they need protein to do it.

Picture this: every rep, every set, and every drop of sweat are investments in your body's future. But without enough protein, those investments won't yield the returns you crave. Protein is the contractor that repairs the damaged muscle tissue, making it thicker, denser, and more powerful than before.

So, what's the deal with protein sources? Well, think of them as different tools in your muscle-building toolbox. Some are tried-and-true classics, while others are versatile newcomers.

- The Classics: Lean meats like chicken, turkey, and beef are your timeless protein allies. They're packed with essential amino acids, the building blocks of muscle. When you're looking to pack on mass, these should be your first choices. They're lean, mean, and muscle-building machines.

- Dairy Delights: Greek yogurt, cottage cheese, and milk are dairy powerhouses that are rich in protein. They also provide valuable calcium and other nutrients. If you're looking for a creamy way to fuel your muscles, these options are worth considering.

- Plant-Based Players: Not a fan of meat or dairy? No problem. Plant-based protein sources like tofu, lentils, chickpeas, and quinoa can be your go-to options. They offer protein with a side of fiber and an array of essential nutrients.

- Protein Powders: In the fast-paced world of bodybuilding, convenience matters. Protein powders, whether whey, casein, or plant-based, are quick and easy sources of protein. They're ideal for post-workout recovery when your muscles are hungry for nutrients.

But here's the deal-breaker – it's not just about the quantity of protein; it's also about the quality. Protein sources vary in terms of amino acid profiles and absorption rates. You want protein sources that are rich in essential amino acids and are easily digestible, ensuring your muscles get the most bang for their buck.

Now, let's talk numbers. How much protein do you need to feed those hungry muscles? The answer depends on various factors, including your body weight, age, activity level, and your specific bodybuilding goals.

For most bodybuilders, a good rule of thumb is to aim for around 1.2 to 2.2 grams of protein per kilogram of body weight daily. This range allows room for customization based on your unique needs. If you're looking to bulk up and pack on muscle, you may lean towards the higher end of the spectrum. If you're in a cutting phase and aiming to shed fat while preserving muscle, the lower end may suffice.

Carbohydrates: The Energy Source

Carbs often get a bad rap in the dieting world, but in the realm of bodybuilding, they're your secret weapon. Carbohydrates are your primary source of energy, the fuel that powers your workouts and recovery.

Picture your body as a high-performance car. It needs the right fuel to perform at its best. Complex carbohydrates are your premium octane. They provide a slow and steady release of energy, keeping you revved up throughout your grueling workouts.

But not all carbs are created equal. You've probably heard of simple carbs and complex carbs. Let's break it down.

- Simple Carbs: These are the sugary, quick-burning carbs found in candy, soda, and other processed junk. They might give you a temporary spike in energy, but they'll leave you crashing and burning soon after.

- Complex Carbs: These are your allies in the quest for muscle. Foods like brown rice, oats, sweet potatoes, wholegrain bread, and legumes provide a sustained release of energy. They keep you going strong, powering through set after set.

Now, here's the kicker – timing matters. Pre-workout nutrition is your opportunity to prime your body for a killer session at the gym. You want a meal or snack that provides a good balance of carbohydrates to fuel your workout and protein to kickstart muscle recovery. Think of it as loading up your car with premium fuel before a race.

Post-workout nutrition is equally crucial. After your intense training session, your muscles are starving for nutrients. This is the time to replenish your glycogen stores with carbohydrates and provide your muscles with the protein they need for recovery and growth. A post-workout shake or a well-balanced meal is your best bet.

But remember, carbohydrates aren't a license to gorge on pizza and pasta. The key is to choose complex carbs that are nutrient-dense and support your bodybuilding goals. You're not just fueling up; you're investing in your body's performance and progress.

- Fats: Essential for Hormone Production

- Fats have long been misunderstood and unfairly demonized in the world of nutrition. But in the world of bodybuilding, they're essential for hormone production, including testosterone, which plays a pivotal role in muscle growth.

- Think of fats as the oil that keeps the gears of your body's engine running smoothly. They're involved in various processes, including nutrient absorption, cell membrane health, and the production of vital hormones. Without enough healthy fats, your bodybuilding journey can hit a roadblock.

- But not all fats are created equal. There are the good guys – healthy fats – and the bad guys – trans fats and excessive saturated fats. Let's focus on the heroes of the story.

- Omega-3 Fatty Acids: Found in fatty fish like salmon, mackerel, and sardines, as well as walnuts and flaxseeds, omega-3 fatty acids are anti-inflammatory powerhouses. They support joint health, reduce muscle soreness, and aid in recovery.

- Monounsaturated Fats: Olive oil, avocados, and nuts are rich in monounsaturated fats. They promote heart health and provide a source of sustainable energy.

- Polyunsaturated Fats: These fats, found in sources like sunflower seeds, soybean oil, and fatty fish, are essential for overall health. They're also involved in maintaining the integrity of cell membranes.

Healthy fats not only keep your body's engine running but also aid in the absorption of fat-soluble vitamins like A, D, E, and K. So, when you're crafting your bodybuilding diet, don't skimp on fats; choose wisely.

Micronutrients and Supplements

In the unrelenting world of bodybuilding, where every lift, every repetition, and every drop of sweat counts, micronutrients and supplements are the secret arsenal that can elevate your journey to unprecedented heights. This chapter, "Micronutrients and Supplements," is not about the mainstream hype or miracle pills; it's about the nitty-gritty essentials that can make or break your pursuit of the ultimate physique.

Vitamins and Minerals for Muscle Health

Let's kick things off with the unsung heroes of nutrition – vitamins and minerals. Often overlooked in favor of macronutrients, these micronutrients are the foundation of your body's intricate machinery. They're the nuts and bolts that keep everything running smoothly.

- Vitamin A: Essential for maintaining healthy skin and mucous membranes, vitamin A also supports vision and immune function. It's found in foods like sweet potatoes, carrots, and spinach.

- Vitamin D: Known as the sunshine vitamin, vitamin D plays a crucial role in calcium absorption, bone health, and immune function. Get your fix from sunlight or fortified foods like fatty fish and fortified dairy products.

- Vitamin C: This antioxidant powerhouse supports collagen production, aids in wound healing, and boosts the immune system. Citrus fruits, strawberries, and bell peppers are excellent sources.

- Vitamin E: With its antioxidant properties, vitamin E helps protect cells from oxidative damage. Nuts, seeds, and vegetable oils are rich sources.

- Vitamin K: Vital for blood clotting and bone metabolism, vitamin K is found in leafy greens like kale, spinach, and broccoli.

- B Vitamins: This group includes B1 (thiamine), B2 (riboflavin), B3 (niacin), B5 (pantothenic acid), B6 (pyridoxine), B7 (biotin), B9 (folate), and B12 (cobalamin). They're involved in energy metabolism, red blood cell formation, and various cellular processes. Whole grains, meat, dairy, and leafy greens are good sources.

- Calcium: Essential for strong bones and muscle function, calcium can be found in dairy products, leafy greens, and fortified foods.

- Iron: Crucial for oxygen transport in the blood and muscle function, iron is abundant in red meat, poultry, fish, and legumes.

- Magnesium: This mineral is involved in muscle contraction and relaxation, energy production, and bone health. You can find it in nuts, seeds, whole grains, and leafy greens.

- Zinc: Essential for immune function and protein synthesis, zinc is prevalent in meat, dairy, nuts, and legumes.

- Selenium: An antioxidant that supports thyroid function and immune health, selenium is found in nuts, seeds, and seafood.

- Potassium: Crucial for muscle contractions and nerve impulses, potassium is abundant in bananas, potatoes, and citrus fruits.

These micronutrients aren't just fancy buzzwords. They're the vitamins and minerals your body needs to operate at peak performance. They're not optional; they're mandatory for the meticulous process of sculpting muscle and achieving your bodybuilding goals. Deficiencies can derail your progress faster than you can say "biceps."

The Role of Supplements

Now, let's talk about supplements – those pills, powders, and potions that promise to take your gains to the next level. Supplements can be a valuable addition to your bodybuilding toolkit, but they're not magic bullets. It's crucial to understand their role and use them wisely.

- Pre-Workout Supplements: These are designed to boost energy, focus, and endurance before hitting the gym. They often contain caffeine, creatine, and amino acids. While they can provide a temporary performance boost, they're not a substitute for a solid nutrition plan and should be used in moderation.

- Protein Supplements: Protein shakes and powders are convenient sources of protein, especially post-workout when your muscles need it the most. They're not a replacement for whole-food sources of protein but can be a useful tool for meeting your daily protein intake goals.

- Recovery Supplements: Branched-Chain Amino Acids (BCAAs) and glutamine are often marketed as recovery aids. While there's some evidence to suggest they may reduce muscle soreness and support recovery, they should complement a well-rounded diet rather than replace it.

- Vitamins and Minerals: If you have specific micronutrient deficiencies or struggle to meet your daily requirements through food alone, multivitamin and mineral supplements can be a safety net. However, it's best to get your nutrients from whole foods whenever possible.

- Fish Oil: Omega-3 fatty acids, found in fish oil supplements, have anti-inflammatory properties and can support joint and heart health. If you don't consume fatty fish regularly, consider this supplement.

- Creatine: Creatine is one of the most researched and proven supplements for increasing muscle mass and strength. It enhances ATP production, which can lead to improved performance during high-intensity, short-duration activities like weightlifting.

- Caffeine: Caffeine can increase alertness and energy levels, potentially improving workout performance. However, its effects can vary from person to person, and excessive caffeine intake can lead to negative side effects.

It's crucial to approach supplements with caution. While they can provide benefits, they should never replace a balanced diet rich in whole foods. Supplements are meant to supplement your nutrition, not substitute it. Before adding any supplement to your regimen, consult with a healthcare professional to ensure it's safe and suitable for your specific needs and goals.

Potential Risks and Benefits

In the quest for bodybuilding glory, it's tempting to view supplements as shortcuts to success. However, it's essential to weigh the potential risks against the benefits, especially when it comes to the unregulated supplement industry.

Benefits:

Convenience: Supplements can be a convenient way to meet your nutritional needs, especially when you're on the go or need a quick protein fix post-workout.

Performance Enhancement: Some supplements, like creatine, caffeine, and BCAAs, may enhance performance and recovery, allowing you to push harder in the gym.

Micronutrient Insurance: Multivitamin supplements can provide a safety net to cover potential micronutrient gaps in your diet.

Risks:

Quality Control: The supplement industry is notorious for poor quality control and mislabeling. Not all supplements contain what they claim, and some may even be contaminated with harmful substances.

Dependency: Relying too heavily on supplements can lead to a dependency mindset, neglecting the importance of whole foods in your diet.

Side Effects: Some supplements can cause adverse side effects or interact with medications. It's crucial to research and consult a healthcare professional before adding them to your regimen.

Financial Cost: Quality supplements can be expensive, and the cost can add up quickly if you're not careful.

In the end, the decision to use supplements should be a calculated one, based on your individual needs, goals, and the potential benefits they offer. Remember that no supplement can replace the foundation of proper nutrition, consistency in training, and restorative sleep.

Meal Planning and Timing

In the world of bodybuilding, where the pursuit of strength and aesthetics demands discipline and precision, the battle isn't just fought in the gym. It's waged on your plate, with every morsel of food, and every sip of liquid you consume. This chapter, "Meal Planning and Timing," is the blueprint for optimizing your nutrition strategy, ensuring that you fuel your body for peak performance and muscle growth without faltering in the face of dietary chaos.

The Importance of Meal Timing

In the battlefield of bodybuilding, timing is everything. It's not just about what you eat, but when you eat it. You wouldn't go to war without a strategy, and you shouldn't embark on your bodybuilding journey without a meal timing plan.

Pre-Workout Nutrition

Picture this: you're gearing up for a brutal training session, ready to unleash your inner beast on the weights. But there's an essential task at hand – fueling your body for the impending battle.

Pre-workout nutrition is your ticket to peak performance. It's about supplying your body with the right nutrients to ensure that you have the energy, focus, and strength needed to conquer your workout. The goal is simple: maximize your output in the gym, and you'll maximize your results.

Here's the breakdown:

Carbohydrates: Complex carbohydrates are your primary source of pre-workout fuel. They provide a steady release of energy to keep you going throughout your session. Think of them as the slow-burning fire that sustains your workout intensity.

Protein: While carbohydrates are the main event, protein plays a supporting role in pre-workout nutrition. It provides amino acids that help prevent muscle breakdown during your training session. It's like having body armor for your muscles.

Fats: Although fats aren't a primary focus of pre-workout nutrition, they can provide some sustained energy. However, keep fat intake moderate to avoid digestive discomfort during your workout.

Hydration: Hydration is non-negotiable. Dehydration can lead to decreased performance, fatigue, and even muscle cramps. Start your workout well-hydrated, and consider sipping on water or an electrolyte drink during your training.

The timing of your pre-workout meal or snack matters. You want to eat about 1 to 2 hours before hitting the gym, allowing your body to digest and absorb the nutrients effectively. If you're in a rush, a smaller snack 30 minutes before your workout can still provide a boost.

So, what does a pre-workout meal or snack look like in the real world?

Example Pre-Workout Meals:

- Grilled chicken breast with brown rice and steamed broccoli: A classic bodybuilder's choice, providing a balance of protein, complex carbs, and fiber for sustained energy.

- Greek yogurt with berries and a drizzle of honey: A quick and easy option rich in protein and carbohydrates.

- Oatmeal with sliced banana and a scoop of protein powder: A hearty meal with a blend of complex carbs and protein.

- Whole-grain toast with almond butter and a sprinkle of cinnamon: A simple yet effective choice that provides energy without being too heavy.

The key is to experiment and find what works best for you. Some people prefer a solid meal, while others opt for a light snack. Pay attention to how your body responds and adjust accordingly.

Intra-Workout Nutrition

During your intense training session, your muscles are working at full throttle, demanding fuel to sustain their performance. While you don't need a full-blown meal mid-workout, some strategic choices can keep your energy levels stable and support muscle recovery.

- Carbohydrate Sources: If your workout is exceptionally long or intense, consider sipping on a carbohydrate-based sports drink or consuming a carbohydrate gel to replenish glycogen stores and maintain energy levels.

- Amino Acids: Branched-Chain Amino Acids (BCAAs) or an essential amino acid supplement can help prevent muscle breakdown during extended workouts.

- Water: Stay hydrated throughout your workout. Dehydration can lead to decreased performance and muscle cramps.

- Intra-workout nutrition isn't always necessary for shorter training sessions, but it can be beneficial for marathon gym sessions or endurance training. Again, it's about customizing your strategy to match your specific needs.

- Post-Workout Nutrition: The Anabolic Window

You've just pushed your body to its limits, breaking down muscle fibers in the process. Now it's time for recovery, and post-workout nutrition is your secret weapon in the battle against muscle soreness and fatigue.

The post-workout period is often referred to as the "anabolic window." It's a window of opportunity when your muscles are primed for nutrient uptake, and the right choices can kick start the repair and growth process.

Here's what you need to know:

Protein: Post-workout, your muscles are hungry for protein. This is the time to provide them with the amino acids they need to rebuild and grow. Whey protein, due to its rapid digestion and absorption, is a popular choice, but other protein sources like lean meats, fish, eggs, or plant-based options work just as well.

Carbohydrates: Carbohydrates play a crucial role in post-workout nutrition as well. They replenish glycogen stores that were depleted during your workout and provide an insulin spike that can enhance protein uptake. Fast-digesting carbohydrates like white rice, potatoes, or simple sugars can be effective choices.

Hydration: Rehydrate with water or an electrolyte drink to replace fluids lost during your workout.

Timing: The post-workout meal or shake should be consumed ideally within 30 minutes to 2 hours after your workout. This timing can maximize the benefits of the anabolic window.

Example Post-Workout Meals:

- Grilled salmon with quinoa and steamed asparagus: A well-rounded meal providing protein, complex carbs, and essential nutrients.

- Protein shake with whey protein, a banana, and a tablespoon of honey: A quick and convenient option that hits the mark for protein and carbohydrates.

- Turkey sandwich on whole-grain bread with plenty of veggies: A balanced choice that combines protein, carbohydrates, and fiber.

- Vegan protein bowl with brown rice, tofu, and mixed vegetables: A plant-based option rich in protein and complex carbs.

Remember that your post-workout meal doesn't need to be overly complicated. The goal is to provide your body with the nutrients it needs for recovery and growth. Tailor your choices to your dietary preferences and sensitivities.

Meal Frequency: The 3-4 Hour Rule

In the world of bodybuilding, consistency is king. It's not just about what you eat but how often you eat. The 3-4 hour rule is a fundamental principle of meal frequency for bodybuilders. Here's how it works:

- Eat Every 3-4 Hours: You should aim to eat a meal or snack every 3-4 hours throughout the day. This consistent meal frequency helps maintain a steady supply of nutrients to support muscle growth and recovery.

- Prevents Muscle Breakdown: Eating regularly prevents your body from going into a catabolic state, where it breaks down muscle tissue for energy. By providing a constant stream of nutrients, you keep your muscles in an anabolic, or growth-promoting, state.

- Optimizes Nutrient Timing: The 3-4 hour rule aligns with the timing of your workouts. By having a meal or snack within a few hours of training, you ensure that your body has the necessary fuel to perform at its best during exercise. Post-workout, another meal or snack replenishes glycogen stores and provides the amino acids needed for muscle repair and growth.

- Balances Blood Sugar: Consistent meal frequency helps stabilize blood sugar levels. Sharp spikes and crashes in blood sugar can lead to cravings, mood swings, and energy slumps. By eating every 3-4 hours, you maintain steady energy levels and reduce the risk of overindulging in unhealthy snacks.

- Supports Metabolism: Regular meals and snacks keep your metabolism revved up. Your body burns calories while digesting and processing food, and frequent eating helps maintain this calorie-burning process throughout the day.

- Prevents Overeating: When you allow too much time between meals, you're more likely to become ravenous and overeat during your next meal. By eating every 3-4 hours, you can better control portion sizes and make healthier food choices.

- Promotes Hydration: Meal frequency also encourages regular hydration. Many bodybuilders forget that water intake is as crucial as food. By eating frequently, you're reminded to stay hydrated, supporting digestion and overall health.

- Creates Routine and Structure: Consistency in meal frequency creates a structured daily routine. This structure can help you plan your workouts, meals, and other activities, making it easier to stay on track with your bodybuilding goals.

- Now, while the 3-4 hour rule is a solid guideline, it's essential to adapt it to your individual needs and schedule. Some people may thrive with more frequent meals, while others may find three main meals and a couple of snacks to be sufficient. The key is to listen to your body and ensure you're meeting your daily calorie and nutrient requirements.

- Incorporate lean proteins, complex carbohydrates, and healthy fats into your meals and snacks to support muscle growth, energy, and overall health. Remember that portion control is vital, even when eating frequently, to avoid excessive calorie intake.

- Consistency is the cornerstone of success in bodybuilding. Whether you're in the bulking or cutting phase, adhering to a regular meal frequency is a non-negotiable part of your nutrition strategy. Embrace the 3-4 hour rule as a fundamental principle in your bodybuilding journey, and watch how it contributes to your progress, one meal at a time.

Nutritional Strategies for Bulking and Cutting

The chapter at hand, "Nutritional Strategies for Bulking and Cutting," is the unwavering blueprint for sculpting your physique, whether you're adding mass or chiseling it to perfection. It's not about following the latest fad or blindly cramming calories; it's about calculated and ruthless nutrition tactics that will propel you towards your bodybuilding goals.

The Bulking Phase: Building the Foundation of Power

Bulking isn't about mindlessly gorging on everything in sight. It's a calculated and strategic approach to building muscle and strength. In this phase, you're in a caloric surplus, consuming more calories than your body burns. The goal is to provide your muscles with an abundance of nutrients to fuel growth, repair, and recovery.

- Caloric Surplus: To bulk effectively, you need a surplus of calories. But don't take it as a license to eat everything in sight. The surplus should be controlled, ensuring that the additional calories go towards muscle growth, not fat storage.

- Macronutrient Ratios: While your macros (protein, carbohydrates, and fats) will largely remain the same, you may adjust the ratios slightly. Protein remains crucial for muscle repair, while carbohydrates provide the energy needed to fuel those intense workouts. Healthy fats should be a part of your diet, but their role is supportive, not primary.

- Protein: Aim to maintain a protein intake of around 1.2 to 2.2 grams per kilogram of body weight. Protein is your muscle's best friend, ensuring you recover and grow optimally during the bulking phase.

- Carbohydrates: Carbs should make up a significant portion of your diet, providing energy for your workouts and aiding in muscle recovery. Complex carbohydrates are your allies, delivering sustained energy without the sugar crashes.

- Fats: Healthy fats are essential for overall health, including hormone production, but keep them in moderation. They're supplementary, helping you meet your caloric needs.

- Meal Timing: The 3-4 hour meal frequency rule still applies. Consistent nutrient intake keeps your body in an anabolic state, conducive to muscle growth.

Examples of Bulking Meals:

- Grilled chicken breast with quinoa, roasted sweet potatoes, and a side of steamed broccoli: A balanced meal providing protein, complex carbs, and fiber.

- Whole-grain pasta with lean ground beef and a tomato-based sauce: A hearty meal rich in protein and complex carbs.

- Protein shake with whey protein, oats, banana, and almond butter: A nutrient-dense option for an additional calorie boost.

The Cutting Phase: Chiseling Your Masterpiece

Once you've built the foundation of muscle mass during the bulking phase, it's time to reveal the masterpiece beneath. The cutting phase is all about shedding body fat while preserving your hard-earned muscle. It's a meticulous dance between calorie restriction and macronutrient optimization.

Caloric Deficit: Cutting involves consuming fewer calories than your body burns, creating a caloric deficit. However, it's crucial to strike a balance – too much of a deficit can lead to muscle loss.

Protein: Your protein intake remains high during cutting to preserve muscle mass. Aim for the same protein range as in the bulking phase.

Carbohydrates: Carbs should still be a part of your diet but may be adjusted downward. Focus on complex carbs to keep you feeling full and energized.

Fats: Healthy fats remain in your diet, as they support overall health and hormone balance. They can also aid in satiety during calorie restriction.

Meal Timing: The 3-4 hour rule continues to be your guide during the cutting phase. Consistency in meal frequency is vital to maintain muscle and curb cravings.

Examples of Cutting Meals:

- Grilled salmon with a side of quinoa and steamed asparagus: A lean protein source combined with complex carbs and fiber for satiety.

- Salad with grilled chicken, mixed greens, and a vinaigrette dressing: A low-calorie, high-protein meal that keeps you feeling full.

- Stir-fried tofu with broccoli and brown rice: A plant-based option rich in protein and complex carbs.

Cardio and Training: Cardio can be a valuable tool during the cutting phase to enhance calorie burning. High-intensity interval training (HIIT) is particularly effective for fat loss. However, don't overdo it, as excessive cardio can lead to muscle loss.

Supplements: During cutting, supplements like BCAAs and whey protein can help preserve muscle and manage cravings. Remember, though, supplements are a complement to your diet, not a replacement.

Hydration: Staying hydrated is crucial during cutting, as thirst can sometimes be mistaken for hunger. Drink plenty of water throughout the day.

Tracking Progress: Keep a close eye on your progress during the cutting phase. Regular assessments of body composition, such as body fat percentage and muscle mass, can help you fine-tune your approach.

Cheat Meals: While discipline is essential, occasional cheat meals can be a mental relief and help prevent binging. Keep them controlled and don't let them derail your progress.

Cycling: Some bodybuilders employ calorie cycling during the cutting phase, alternating between higher and lower-calorie days. This approach can help prevent metabolic adaptation and maintain muscle.

Refeeding: Periodic refeeding days, where you temporarily increase your calorie intake, can help reset hormone levels and alleviate some of the metabolic slowdown associated with prolonged calorie restriction.

The key to success in the cutting phase is discipline and consistency. It's not an easy journey, and it demands mental fortitude, but the results are worth the sacrifice. Cutting is about revealing the masterpiece you've sculpted during bulking, and the sharper your tools, the more impeccable your creation will be.

Specialized Diets for Bodybuilders

Nutrition is the unsung hero that separates the champions from the rest. This chapter, "Specialized Diets for Bodybuilders," isn't about quick fixes or trendy diets; it's about ruthless and calculated approaches to nutrition that can take your physique to the next level. If you're ready to push your limits and sculpt your body into a work of art, read on.

Ketogenic Diet: Carving out the Fat

The ketogenic diet, often dubbed "keto," has gained notoriety for its remarkable ability to shed body fat like a hot knife through butter. This high-fat, low-carb diet is a weapon of choice for bodybuilders looking to get leaner while preserving muscle mass.

In a ketogenic diet:

- Carbohydrates are severely restricted: Typically, carbs make up only about 5-10% of total daily calories. This restriction forces your body to rely on fat for fuel instead of glucose from carbs.

- Fats take the spotlight: Approximately 70-80% of your daily calories come from healthy fats like avocados, nuts, seeds, and oils. These fats become the primary energy source.

- Protein remains moderate: Protein intake hovers around 15-20% of daily calories. It's sufficient to support muscle maintenance and growth.

The ketogenic diet induces a state called ketosis, where your body starts producing ketones from fat breakdown. Ketones serve as an alternative fuel source for your muscles and brain. During this process, your body becomes incredibly efficient at burning stored fat for energy, making it an excellent choice for cutting phases.

However, the keto diet isn't a walk in the park. It demands strict adherence, and the initial transition can be mentally and physically challenging as your body adapts to the absence of carbs. It's not a long-term solution, but when used strategically during cutting phases, it can yield remarkable results in shedding body fat while preserving muscle.

Cyclical Ketogenic Diet: The Best of Both Worlds

For those who crave carbohydrates, the cyclical ketogenic diet (CKD) offers a compromise. CKD involves cycling between periods of strict keto and short "carb-loading" phases.

Here's how it works:

- Keto Phase: During this phase, which can last anywhere from 5 to 6 days, you follow a strict ketogenic diet, similar to what was described earlier. Your carb intake is minimal.

- Carb-Loading Phase: This is the break you've been waiting for. On this day (or sometimes two days), you load up on carbs, sometimes exceeding your daily calorie needs. This carb influx refills muscle glycogen stores and provides a mental and physical boost.

CKD offers the metabolic benefits of ketosis while providing periodic relief from carb restriction. It's a strategy favored by some bodybuilders to enjoy the best of both worlds – the fat-shredding power of keto and the muscle-sparing properties of carb refeeds.

Intermittent Fasting: Fasting for Gains

Intermittent fasting (IF) is a nutritional strategy that's gained popularity in recent years, thanks to its simplicity and potential health benefits. For bodybuilders, it can be a valuable tool for managing calorie intake, improving insulin sensitivity, and supporting fat loss.

IF involves cycling between periods of fasting and eating. Here are some common IF approaches:

- 16/8 Method: This method involves fasting for 16 hours each day and limiting your eating window to 8 hours. Most people achieve this by skipping breakfast and eating their first meal around noon.

- 5:2 Method: In this approach, you eat normally for five days of the week and limit calorie intake to around 500-600 calories on the remaining two days.

- Eat-Stop-Eat: With this method, you fast for a full 24 hours once or twice a week. For example, you might eat dinner at 7 pm one day and not eat again until 7 pm the following day.

- Alternate-Day Fasting: This approach involves alternating between days of regular eating and days of fasting or consuming very few calories.

Intermittent fasting isn't about restricting specific food groups or macronutrients; it's about controlling when you eat. During the fasting period, your body taps into stored fat for energy, potentially aiding in fat loss. It can also improve insulin sensitivity, which is beneficial for overall health and muscle growth.

However, IF may not be suitable for everyone, especially those with specific dietary requirements or training schedules. It's essential to tailor the fasting approach to your individual needs and goals.

Vegetarian and Vegan Diets: Plant-Powered Gains

Contrary to the misconception that bodybuilding relies solely on animal protein, vegetarian and vegan diets can also be powerful tools for muscle growth and strength. With careful planning and strategic food choices, plant-powered bodybuilders can achieve remarkable results.

Here's how it's done:

- Protein Sources: Plant-based protein sources become the cornerstone of your diet. These include tofu, tempeh, seitan, legumes (such as lentils, chickpeas, and black beans), and plant-based protein powders. Nuts and seeds are also excellent protein sources.

- Amino Acid Balance: To ensure you're getting all the essential amino acids, it's crucial to diversify your protein sources. Combining different plant proteins, like beans and rice, can help achieve a balanced amino acid profile.

- Iron-Rich Foods: Plant-based diets can provide plenty of iron through foods like dark leafy greens, fortified cereals, and legumes. Iron is essential for oxygen transport, which is crucial during workouts.

- B12 Supplementation: Vitamin B12 is primarily found in animal products, so many vegetarians and vegans need to supplement or consume B12-fortified foods to avoid deficiencies.

- Caloric Surplus: To build muscle, you'll still need a caloric surplus, just like any other bodybuilder. This means consuming more calories than you burn to support muscle growth.

Vegetarian and vegan bodybuilders can enjoy the same benefits as their omnivorous counterparts – increased muscle mass, strength, and improved overall health. With proper planning and a keen eye on nutrient intake, plant-powered bodybuilders can thrive in the gym and on the stage.

Carb Cycling: Timing Your Carbs for Gains

Carb cycling is a strategic approach to nutrition that involves alternating between high-carb and low-carb days. It's a favorite among bodybuilders for optimizing energy levels, supporting muscle growth, and managing body fat.

The premise of carb cycling is straightforward:

- High-Carb Days: On these days, you increase your carbohydrate intake to support intense workouts and refuel muscle glycogen stores. High-carb days are often aligned with your most grueling

Staying Hydrated and Monitoring Progress

In bodybuilding, two crucial elements often take a back seat: hydration and progress monitoring. Neglecting these can be the Achilles' heel that undermines your journey to sculpting the ultimate physique. In this chapter, we'll delve into the unsung heroes of bodybuilding – staying hydrated and monitoring progress. No fluff, no frills, just raw knowledge to elevate your game.

Hydration: The Overlooked Game Changer

Water is the unsung hero of your bodybuilding arsenal. While you're busy counting reps and tracking macros, hydration often slips through the cracks. Yet, it's one of the most critical components of your success. Without proper hydration, your body can't perform at its peak, and your gains will suffer.

The Importance of Hydration

Picture this: you're in the midst of an intense workout, beads of sweat pouring down your face, and your muscles pushing to their limit. Every movement is a testament to your dedication. But there's an often-underestimated factor at play – your hydration status.

Hydration is not just about quenching your thirst; it's about ensuring that your body functions optimally. Here's why it matters:

- Muscle Function: Dehydration can lead to muscle cramps and decreased muscle contractions, hampering your performance.

- Temperature Regulation: Sweating is your body's cooling mechanism. Without sufficient water, you risk overheating, which can be dangerous during intense workouts.

- Energy Levels: Even mild dehydration can lead to fatigue and reduced energy levels, making it harder to push through your training sessions.

- Recovery: Proper hydration is essential for post-workout recovery. It helps transport nutrients to your muscles, aiding in repair and growth.

- Cognitive Function: Dehydration can impair focus and cognitive function, affecting your workout intensity and form.

How Much Water Do You Need?

The age-old advice of drinking eight 8-ounce glasses of water a day is a good starting point for the average person. However, bodybuilders often have greater hydration needs due to their intense training regimens and increased sweat rates.

A more personalized approach is to calculate your water needs based on your body weight. As a general guideline, aim for about 30-35 milliliters of water per kilogram of body weight per day. For example, if you weigh 70 kilograms (154 pounds), you'd need approximately 2,100 to 2,450 milliliters of water daily.

Keep in mind that individual factors like climate, activity level, and sweat rate can affect your hydration requirements. On intense workout days, you may need to drink even more to compensate for fluid loss.

Signs of Dehydration

Detecting dehydration early is crucial to prevent its detrimental effects. Here are some common signs to watch out for:

- Thirst: The most apparent signal that your body needs water.

- Dark Urine: Dark yellow or amber-colored urine is a sign of dehydration. Your urine should be pale yellow.

- Dry Mouth and Skin: Dry or sticky feeling in your mouth and skin can indicate dehydration.

- Fatigue: If you feel unusually tired during your workout or throughout the day, it could be due to dehydration.

- Headache: Dehydration can trigger headaches and migraines.

- Muscle Cramps: Frequent muscle cramps, especially during exercise, may be a sign of inadequate hydration.

Strategies for Staying Hydrated

Now that you understand the importance of hydration let's dive into some strategies to ensure you stay adequately hydrated:

- Drink Throughout the Day: Don't wait until you're thirsty to start drinking. Sip water consistently throughout the day.

- Pre-Workout Hydration: Drink a glass of water about 2 hours before your workout to ensure you start your training session well-hydrated.

- During Workout: Sip on water or an electrolyte drink during your workout, especially if it's intense or lengthy. Electrolyte drinks can help replace lost minerals through sweat.

- Post-Workout Rehydration: After your workout, rehydrate with water or a recovery drink to replace fluid losses.

- Monitor Urine Color: Keep an eye on the color of your urine. If it's pale yellow, you're likely well-hydrated. Dark yellow or amber urine is a sign to drink more water.

- Consider Your Environment: Hot and humid conditions can increase sweat rates, so you'll need to drink more to compensate.

- Electrolytes: If you're sweating excessively, especially in a hot climate, consider incorporating electrolyte drinks or foods high in electrolytes, like bananas or coconut water, into your regimen.

Hydration is the foundation of your bodybuilding journey. It's not an option; it's a necessity. Neglecting it can undermine your hard work and dedication in the gym. So, remember to drink up, even when the iron is calling your name.

Monitoring Progress: Your North Star

In the ruthless world of bodybuilding, progress isn't just a goal; it's the guiding light that keeps you on track. Yet, many aspiring bodybuilders stumble in the dark, not knowing how to navigate their journey. That's where progress monitoring comes in – your North Star in the constellation of gains.

Why Monitor Progress

Imagine setting sail on a treacherous sea without a compass or map. You'd be lost in the vastness, drifting aimlessly. The same holds for bodybuilding. Monitoring your progress is your compass, guiding you through the turbulent waters of training and nutrition.

Here's why it matters:

- Motivation: Tracking your progress can be incredibly motivating. It allows you to see the fruits of your labor and provides a sense of achievement.

- Adjustments: Without monitoring, you're flying blind. Progress tracking helps you identify what's working and what isn't, allowing you to make necessary adjustments to your training and nutrition.

- Plateau Prevention: It's not uncommon to hit plateaus in your bodybuilding journey. Progress monitoring helps you recognize when progress stalls so you can pivot and keep moving forward.

- Accountability: When you're tracking your progress, you're less likely to skip workouts or deviate from your nutrition plan. It creates a sense of accountability to your goals.

What to Monitor

Progress monitoring goes beyond simply stepping on a scale. While body weight is one factor, it's far from the only one. Here's what you should be tracking:

- Body Weight: Your weight can provide insights into changes in muscle mass and body fat. However, it's not the sole indicator of progress, as fluctuations can occur due to various factors.

- Body Measurements: Tracking measurements of key areas like chest, waist, hips, arms, and legs can give you a more comprehensive view of your body's transformation. These measurements can help you identify changes in specific muscle groups and areas where you might be losing fat.

- Body Fat Percentage: Measuring your body fat percentage is crucial for understanding how your body composition is evolving. It's a more accurate reflection of progress than body weight alone, as it accounts for changes in muscle and fat.

- Strength and Performance: Keep a close eye on your strength and performance in the gym. Are you lifting heavier weights, completing more reps, or improving your workout intensity? These improvements signal muscle growth and increased fitness levels.

- Energy Levels: Your energy levels are a valuable indicator of your overall health. As your nutrition and training plan progress, you should experience increased energy and endurance during workouts and throughout the day.

- Recovery and Soreness: Pay attention to how quickly you recover from workouts and the level of soreness you experience. Improved recovery and reduced soreness can indicate that your nutrition plan is supporting muscle repair and growth.

- Mood and Mental Clarity: Nutrition doesn't just affect your body; it has a significant impact on your mind. Monitor changes in mood, mental clarity, and focus. A well-balanced diet can enhance your cognitive function and overall well-being.

- Sleep Quality: Adequate sleep is essential for recovery and muscle growth. Track your sleep quality and duration. Improved sleep patterns are a positive sign that your nutrition and training are on the right track.

- Skin Health: The condition of your skin can also reflect your nutritional status. Healthy, clear skin can be a sign of a well-balanced diet with adequate hydration.

- Hunger and Appetite: Pay attention to your hunger and appetite cues. A well-structured nutrition plan should help regulate your appetite and reduce cravings for unhealthy foods.

- Digestive Health: Digestive issues can hinder nutrient absorption. Monitor your digestive health and make adjustments to your diet if you experience discomfort, bloating, or irregularity.

- While these indicators are essential for tracking progress, remember that changes won't happen overnight. Patience and consistency are your allies on this journey. Use these markers to make informed adjustments to your nutrition plan and training regimen as you work toward your bodybuilding goals. The path to mastery is marked by these small steps and incremental improvements, and every bit of progress is a step closer to the body you're sculpting.

Example Meal Plans

In this chapter, we won't delve into the intricacies of theory or dabble in the hypothetical; we'll cut through the noise and lay bare the practicality of nutrition mastery with concrete example meal plans. No frills, no fluff, just the battle-tested fuel that will propel you closer to your bodybuilding goals.

Meal Plan 1: Fuel for Bulking

Bulking isn't an invitation for reckless eating; it's a calculated assault on muscle growth. Here's a meal plan that provides the sustenance needed to add mass without sacrificing quality.

Meal 1: Breakfast

- Scrambled Eggs: 3 large eggs cooked in olive oil for healthy fats and protein.
- Whole-Grain Toast: 2 slices for complex carbs and fiber.
- Spinach and Tomato: A side of veggies for vitamins and minerals.

Meal 2: Mid-Morning Snack

- Greek Yogurt: 1 cup for protein and probiotics.
- Mixed Berries: A handful for antioxidants and flavor.

Meal 3: Lunch

- Grilled Chicken Breast: 6 ounces for lean protein.

- Quinoa: 1 cup for complex carbs and fiber.
- Steamed Broccoli: A side of greens for nutrients.

Meal 4: Pre-Workout

- Protein Shake: 1 scoop of whey protein for fast-digesting amino acids.
- Banana: A quick source of energy.

Meal 5: Post-Workout

- Salmon: 6 ounces for protein and healthy fats.
- Brown Rice: 1 cup for sustained energy.
- Asparagus: A side of greens for vitamins and fiber.

Meal 6: Dinner

- Lean Beef Steak: 6 ounces for protein and iron.
- Sweet Potatoes: 1 cup for complex carbs and beta-carotene.
- Mixed Vegetables: A side of colorful veggies for vitamins.

Meal 7: Evening Snack

- Cottage Cheese: 1 cup for casein protein (slow-digesting).
- Almonds: A small handful for healthy fats.

Meal Plan 2: Precision for Cutting

Cutting is about sculpting your masterpiece by shedding excess body fat while preserving muscle. This meal plan provides the precision needed to reveal the chiseled physique beneath.

Meal 1: Breakfast

- Oatmeal: 1 cup for complex carbs and fiber.
- Egg Whites: 4 egg whites for protein.
- Spinach: A handful for added nutrients.

Meal 2: Mid-Morning Snack

- Protein Shake: 1 scoop of whey protein.
- Almonds: A small handful for healthy fats.

Meal 3: Lunch

- Grilled Turkey Breast: 6 ounces for lean protein.
- Quinoa Salad: 1 cup for complex carbs and fiber.
- Mixed Greens: A generous portion for vitamins.

Meal 4: Pre-Workout

- Greek Yogurt: 1 cup for protein.
- Berries: A handful for antioxidants.

Meal 5: Post-Workout

- Chicken Breast: 6 ounces for lean protein.
- Brown Rice: 1 cup for complex carbs.
- Broccoli: A side of greens for vitamins and fiber.

Meal 6: Dinner

- Salmon: 6 ounces for protein and healthy fats.

- Asparagus: A side of greens for nutrients.
- Quinoa: 1/2 cup for additional carbs.

Meal 7: Evening Snack

- Cottage Cheese: 1 cup for casein protein.
- Walnuts: A small handful for healthy fats.

Meal Plan 3: Vegetarian Power

Contrary to the misconception that bodybuilding relies solely on animal protein, a vegetarian meal plan can provide the power needed for muscle growth and strength.

Meal 1: Breakfast

- Scrambled Tofu: Tofu cooked with veggies for protein and nutrients.
- Whole-Grain Toast: 2 slices for complex carbs.
- Spinach and Tomato: A side of greens for vitamins.

Meal 2: Mid-Morning Snack

- Greek Yogurt: 1 cup for protein.
- Mixed Berries: A handful for antioxidants.

Meal 3: Lunch

- Tempeh Stir-Fry: Tempeh with mixed vegetables for protein and fiber.
- Brown Rice: 1 cup for complex carbs.

Meal 4: Pre-Workout

- Protein Shake: 1 scoop of plant-based protein.
- Banana: A quick source of energy.

Meal 5: Post-Workout

- Chickpea Salad: Chickpeas with veggies for protein and fiber.
- Quinoa: 1/2 cup for additional carbs.

Meal 6: Dinner

- Lentil Curry: Lentils cooked with spices and served with brown rice for protein and complex carbs.
- Mixed Vegetables: A side of greens for vitamins.

Meal 7: Evening Snack

- Cottage Cheese: 1 cup for casein protein.
- Almonds: A small handful for healthy fats.

These meal plans are not set in stone but serve as templates to demonstrate the practicality of a balanced nutrition strategy. The key to success is consistency and adaptability. Tailor your meals to your preferences and dietary requirements while adhering to your macro and calorie targets. Remember, nutrition mastery is about the relentless pursuit of your bodybuilding goals, one meal at a time.

Common Mistakes and Pitfalls

In the relentless pursuit of the perfect physique, where sweat and iron are your constant companions, there's little room for error. Yet, even the most dedicated bodybuilders can stumble and fall prey to common mistakes and pitfalls along the way. In this chapter, we'll expose these pitfalls, not to dwell on them, but to arm you with the knowledge to sidestep these traps and keep forging ahead.

Neglecting Proper Warm-Ups and Cool-Downs

Picture this: you walk into the gym, fueled with determination, ready to conquer the weights. You head straight to the squat rack, load up the bar, and dive into your working sets. Sounds familiar? It's a common scenario, but it's also a recipe for disaster.

The Mistake: Neglecting proper warm-ups and cool-downs.

Why It's a Pitfall: Failing to warm up adequately can increase the risk of injuries and reduce your performance during your workout. Conversely, skipping a cool-down can lead to delayed onset muscle soreness (DOMS) and hinder recovery.

The Solution: Prioritize your warm-up and cool-down routines. Start with 5-10 minutes of light aerobic activity to increase blood flow to your muscles. Follow it with dynamic stretching or mobility exercises to prepare your body for the workout ahead. After your workout, dedicate another 5-10 minutes to static stretching and foam rolling to aid recovery.

Overtraining and Under-Recovery

In the pursuit of gains, more is not always better. Many bodybuilders fall victim to the belief that relentless training and minimal rest will accelerate progress. However, this approach can lead to a vicious cycle of overtraining and under-recovery.

The Mistake: Overtraining and neglecting the importance of recovery.

Why It's a Pitfall: Overtraining can lead to fatigue, decreased performance, increased risk of injuries, and even hormonal imbalances. It hampers your body's ability to repair and grow muscle.

The Solution: Prioritize rest and recovery as much as your training sessions. Ensure you're getting adequate sleep, as it's during slumber that your body performs its most significant recovery and repair work. Implement planned deload weeks in your training program to allow your body to recuperate fully. Listen to your body; if you're feeling excessively fatigued or experiencing chronic soreness, it's a sign to ease up and prioritize recovery.

Ignoring Proper Form

In the world of bodybuilding, lifting heavy is a badge of honor. However, this pursuit of weightlifting supremacy can often come at the expense of proper form and technique.

The Mistake: Ignoring proper form and prioritizing lifting heavier weights.

Why It's a Pitfall: Neglecting form can lead to injuries and limit muscle activation. It shifts the focus from targeted muscle groups to secondary muscles, reducing the effectiveness of your exercises.

The Solution: Prioritize proper form above all else. Focus on controlled, full-range-of-motion repetitions. Reduce the weight if needed to maintain good form. If you're unsure about your technique, seek guidance from a qualified trainer or use mirrors to visually assess your form during exercises.

Neglecting Nutrient Timing

Nutrition is the lifeblood of bodybuilding, and timing plays a crucial role in optimizing your results. Yet, many bodybuilders overlook the significance of nutrient timing, missing out on the full potential of their nutrition strategy.

The Mistake: Neglecting nutrient timing, such as pre-workout and post-workout nutrition.

Why It's a Pitfall: Timing your nutrients strategically can enhance workout performance, muscle recovery, and growth. Neglecting this aspect can leave gains on the table.

The Solution: Prioritize pre-workout and post-workout nutrition. Consume a balanced meal or snack 1-2 hours before your workout, focusing on a combination of carbohydrates and protein. After your workout, have a post-workout meal or shake within 30 minutes to 2 hours, emphasizing protein and fast-digesting carbohydrates to kickstart recovery.

Excessive Supplementation

The supplement industry is a billion-dollar business, and it's easy to fall into the trap of believing that a cabinet full of pills and powders will be the key to your success.

The Mistake: Relying too heavily on supplements.

Why It's a Pitfall: Supplements are meant to complement your diet, not replace it. Depending on supplements can lead to nutrient imbalances and financial strain.

The Solution: Prioritize whole foods as the foundation of your nutrition. Supplements should be used strategically to fill gaps in your diet, not as a primary source of nutrients. Focus on essentials like protein powder, creatine, and branched-chain amino acids (BCAAs), but don't neglect a well-balanced diet.

Inconsistent Tracking

In the world of bodybuilding, consistency is king. Whether it's tracking your workouts, nutrition, or progress, inconsistency can lead to stagnation.

The Mistake: Inconsistent tracking of workouts, nutrition, and progress.

Why It's a Pitfall: Inconsistency makes it challenging to identify what's working and what isn't. It hinders your ability to make informed adjustments to your training and nutrition plan.

The Solution: Prioritize consistency in tracking. Keep a detailed workout journal, recording exercises, sets, reps, and weights. Track your daily nutrition intake, including macros and calories. Take regular progress photos and measurements to monitor changes in your physique. This data will be invaluable in fine-tuning your approach and ensuring steady progress.

Neglecting Mobility and Flexibility

In the quest for muscle and strength, flexibility and mobility are often disregarded. However, these aspects are crucial for injury prevention and optimal performance.

The Mistake: Neglecting mobility and flexibility training.

Why It's a Pitfall: Poor mobility and flexibility can lead to imbalances, reduced range of motion, and an increased risk of injuries. It can also hinder your ability to perform exercises with proper form.

The Solution: Prioritize mobility and flexibility exercises in your routine. Include dynamic stretches and mobility drills in your warm-up to prepare your muscles and joints for exercise. Dedicate time to static stretching and foam rolling in your cool-down to enhance flexibility and aid recovery.

Progress isn't always a linear path. You'll encounter setbacks, challenges, and moments of self-doubt. However, by learning from the common mistakes and pitfalls that many bodybuilders face, you can navigate your journey with greater confidence and success.

Remember, it's not about avoiding these pitfalls entirely; it's about recognizing them, learning from them, and using them as stepping stones toward your ultimate goal: mastery of your body and your craft.

Mental and Emotional Aspects

In the relentless and unforgiving world of bodybuilding, where iron meets sweat and ambition knows no bounds, the focus has always been on the physical. Countless repetitions, meticulously calculated macronutrients, and unwavering dedication are the hallmarks of success. But in the pursuit of the perfect physique, there's a critical aspect that often goes overlooked: the mental and emotional dimensions of this grueling journey.

The Mindset of a Champion

While the weights themselves may not change, the mindset of a bodybuilder can be the difference between mediocrity and greatness. Your mental approach to training, nutrition, and competition can be a formidable weapon in your arsenal.

1. Discipline and Consistency: The bedrock of bodybuilding success is discipline. It's the relentless commitment to your training and nutrition regimen, day in and day out, even when motivation wanes. True champions understand that progress is built on consistency, not just on the days when you feel inspired but every single day.

2. Resilience in the Face of Setbacks: Injuries, plateaus, and unexpected setbacks are an inevitable part of the bodybuilding journey. What separates the elite from the rest is their ability to adapt and overcome. A setback is not a defeat; it's a challenge to conquer. Resilience is the ability to bounce back stronger than ever.

3. Mental Toughness: The weights don't care if you're having a bad day or if life is throwing curveballs your way. Mental toughness is

the ability to push through those tough moments, to complete that last rep when your muscles scream, and to stay on track when temptation lurks around every corner.

4. Goal Setting and Visualization: Successful bodybuilders are not just lifting weights; they're lifting themselves toward a vision of their ideal physique. Setting clear, realistic goals and visualizing success are powerful tools to keep you motivated and on track.

5. Mind-Muscle Connection: Beyond lifting heavy, the ability to establish a deep mind-muscle connection is what separates bodybuilders from mere weightlifters. It's about feeling every contraction, every stretch, and every fiber of your muscles working. A focused mind enhances the effectiveness of your workouts.

The Dark Side of the Mind

While a strong mindset can propel you forward, the journey can also take a toll on your mental and emotional well-being. The relentless pursuit of perfection can become an obsession, leading to negative consequences.

1. Body Dysmorphia: Body dysmorphic disorder is a condition where individuals obsessively focus on perceived flaws in their physical appearance. Bodybuilders are not immune to this. What may begin as a healthy pursuit of a better physique can spiral into a never-ending quest for an unattainable ideal.

2. Disordered Eating: The strict dietary demands of bodybuilding can sometimes lead to disordered eating habits. Preoccupation with food, extreme calorie restriction, or binge-eating episodes can have serious physical and psychological consequences.

3. Social Isolation: The commitment required for bodybuilding often leads to social isolation. Late-night workouts, meal prep, and the sheer physical exhaustion can strain relationships and limit social interactions.

4. Burnout: The relentless nature of the sport can lead to burnout. Overtraining, physical exhaustion, and mental fatigue can sap your motivation and leave you questioning the very pursuit you once loved.

Maintaining Balance

So, how do you navigate the mental and emotional rollercoaster of bodybuilding while staying true to your goals? It's all about balance and self-awareness.

1. Self-Reflection: Regular self-reflection is essential. Take time to assess your motivations and emotional state. Are you enjoying the journey, or has it become a burden? Are you setting realistic goals, or are you chasing an unrealistic ideal? Self-awareness is the first step to addressing any issues.

2. Seek Support: You don't have to go it alone. Share your goals and concerns with a trusted friend, family member, or coach. Having a support system can provide much-needed perspective and emotional support.

3. Professional Help: If you find yourself struggling with body image issues, disordered eating, or severe emotional distress, don't hesitate to seek professional help. Therapists and counselors can provide valuable guidance and support.

4. Rest and Recovery: Your mental and emotional well-being are intrinsically linked to physical rest and recovery. Ensure you're getting enough sleep and taking regular breaks to recharge both physically and mentally.

5. Diversify Your Identity: While bodybuilding may be a significant part of your life, it shouldn't be your entire identity. Cultivate other interests and passions that provide balance and fulfillment.

6. Enjoy the Journey: Remember why you started this journey in the first place – the love for the process, the joy of progress, and the satisfaction of pushing your limits. Enjoy every small victory along the way.

Embracing the Mental and Emotional Struggle

The bodybuilding journey is not for the faint of heart. It's a relentless pursuit that tests your physical, mental, and emotional limits. It's a journey of self-discovery, where you'll encounter both triumphs and tribulations.

In the world of bodybuilding, there is no room for complacency, and the battle is fought on multiple fronts. Beyond the weights and nutrition plans, it's your mindset, your resilience, and your ability to maintain balance that will ultimately determine your success.

Embrace the mental and emotional struggle as an integral part of your journey. It's not a tapestry of perfection but a raw, unfiltered story of determination, passion, and the relentless pursuit of your best self.

Embracing Your Fitness Journey

The world of fitness and bodybuilding is rich with various methodologies and strategies, among which workout splits have emerged as a key element in structuring effective fitness programs. These splits, each with its unique characteristics and benefits, offer diverse ways to organize training to achieve optimal results. The purpose of this chapter is not only to summarize the key takeaways from an exploration of these splits but also to underscore the importance of choosing a workout split that aligns with one's individual goals, lifestyle, and physical capabilities.

Understanding Splits

Workout splits are foundational to structured fitness programs, providing a systematic approach to training. The concept of a split involves dividing your workout routine to focus on different muscle groups or types of exercise on different days. This approach is instrumental in allowing specific muscle recovery while others are being worked, leading to more efficient and productive training sessions. Each type of split, from full-body routines to more specialized regimens like the bro split or the 5x5 program, caters to different training needs and preferences.

Diversity of Splits

The diversity of workout splits is a testament to the variety within fitness training methodologies. Each split, be it a full-body split, upper/lower split, push/pull/legs split, bro split, or the 5x5 program, has unique characteristics that make it suitable for different fitness goals and preferences. For example, full-body splits are great for beginners or those with limited time for workouts, as they allow for a comprehensive workout in each session. On the other hand, more specialized splits like the bro split or the 5x5 program are tailored for those focusing on specific goals like muscle hypertrophy or strength building.

Importance of Nutrition and Recovery

A successful fitness regimen is more than just well-structured workouts; it also involves proper nutrition and recovery. Nutrition plays a critical role in fueling workouts and aiding recovery. A balanced diet, rich in protein, carbohydrates, fats, vitamins, and minerals, supports muscle growth and repair. Hydration is equally important, as water plays a key role in numerous bodily functions, including muscle recovery. Recovery, encompassing both rest days and sleep, is crucial for muscle growth and preventing overtraining. Each workout split should be complemented with a focus on nutrition and recovery for maximum effectiveness.

Adaptability of Splits

The adaptability of workout splits is crucial in their effectiveness. The best workout split is one that fits an individual's lifestyle, personal goals, and physical condition. This adaptability means that a workout routine can be modified as goals change, as one progresses in their fitness journey, or as life circumstances evolve. An individual might start with a full-body split and later transition to a more specialized split as they become more experienced and their goals become more defined.

Experimentation and Evolution

Experimentation is key in finding the most effective workout split. It's important to try different splits to understand what works best for your body and goals. Personal preference plays a significant role in adherence to a fitness regimen, and experimenting with different splits can help identify what is most enjoyable and sustainable for you. As your fitness level evolves, so should your workout split. Being open to modifying your routine as you progress or as your goals change is essential for continued growth and development.

The Role of Guidance and Self-Education

While a thorough understanding of workout splits provides a solid foundation, the value of professional guidance and continued self-education should not be underestimated. Consulting with fitness professionals can provide personalized advice and adjustments to your workout routine. Additionally, continually educating yourself about new training methods, exercises, and nutrition can enhance your fitness journey, making it more effective and enjoyable.

Embracing the Fitness Journey

Finally, it's important to remember that fitness is not just a destination but a journey. It's about enjoying the process, celebrating small victories, and learning from challenges. Your choice of workout split should not only be about achieving your fitness goals but also about enhancing your overall journey, making it more enjoyable and sustainable. Whether you're a beginner or an experienced athlete, the right workout split can be a powerful tool in achieving your fitness goals while keeping the journey rewarding and fulfilling.

Printed in Great Britain
by Amazon